Reviews

In this evocative book, Hari and Subramanian capture the ethos and reasons behind the success of Bigbasket. A seasoned founding team, humility and collaboration and an eye for detail have catapulted Bigbasket into the front line of India's online grocery market. I would strongly recommend this as a must-read for all aspiring as well as established entrepreneurs.

Nandan Nilekani, *Chairman, Infosys, and Chairman and Co-founder, Fundamentum*

Makes for a captivating read! Recommended for everyone interested in start-ups and business. A story of how India is being transformed by entrepreneurial chutzpah. The book contains tonnes of real-life anecdotes and fascinating insights from the creation of one of modern Indian economy's admired businesses.

K. Ganesh, *Serial Entrepreneur and Chairman, GrowthStory*

This is a great story of a company that stuck to the basics of building a sound business. Besides some good learnings, the storytelling style makes the book a delightful read. I would strongly recommend this to everyone who is a part of the start-up ecosystem.

Sanjeev Bikhchandani, *Founder and Executive Vice-Chairman, Naukri*

This book vividly captures the vision, culture and commitment to values, which has made Bigbasket one of India's most successful start-ups. The narrative is laced with several interesting anecdotes, which give us an insight into the highly challenging and complex online grocery business. It boldly lays bare the secret sauce of Bigbasket's success, making it a compelling read. I would urge everyone to read this story.

Rishad Premji, ***Executive Chairman, Wipro***

A very honest ringside account of how a unicorn was created. I was particularly impressed with the emphasis on values, culture and talent; these soft factors make all the difference in determining how far a company will go.

Ravi Venkatesan, ***Member of the Board of Trustees, Rockefeller Foundation, and Founder, Global Alliance for Mass Entrepreneurship***

A riveting book that is very inspiring too. It highlights the need to stay grounded, get the basics right and focus on creating a superlative customer experience. It also highlights the need to relentlessly pursue your goals despite all the many challenges. I hope the book inspires many more entrepreneurs, as India needs more job creators, and start-ups and SMEs will be the job engines of the future.

T.V. Narendran, ***Global CEO and Managing Director, Tata Steel***

This is one of the best books I have read about the journey of a start-up. It has something to offer to everyone in the start-up ecosystem—be it founders, employees, wannabe entrepreneurs or investors. The story narrating style is great and things have been presented the way they are instead of trying to glorify the founders or any single individual or that lone insight. The near-maniacal focus on customer delight is the underlying thread in almost all the chapters, which is a big lesson for everyone. I haven't come across a book that talks about the employees (so many) and gives them as much credit as this book does. The book proves that a company is as good as the broader team, not just the founders. I thoroughly enjoyed reading the book. I would strongly recommend this book to everyone in the start-up ecosystem.

Raghunandan G., *Co-founder, TaxiForSure*

The book is a compelling story of people and processes that have shaped Bigbasket over the years. Every character in the book comes to life as a real person. Everything that seems mundane begins to emerge as 'spectacular' as you unravel the company's journey from a small set-up to one that achieved rapid scale by embracing human-centric innovation. Each section is a honeycomb. Stories are nested in stories and crack open to reveal anecdotes about people, habits, business decisions and innovative practices that worked. The story invites you to be a 'part of it'. The book is inspiring and would appeal to any reader, particularly business enthusiasts.

Gayathri Vasudevan, *Co-founder and CEO, LabourNet*

The book makes for extremely easy reading and offers a very wide range of insights about customer centricity, people, processes, culture, etc. It is a great story and perhaps the first-of-a-kind book about a start-up in India. One can actually live through the first seven years of Bigbasket through this book. I found the book gripping and read it in just two sittings.

Phanindra Sama, *Chief Innovation Officer, Government of Telangana, and Co-founder and former CEO, RedBus*

This is the fascinating success story of a unique start-up that stuck to its mission single-mindedly, took no shortcuts, innovated constantly to increase customer delight and also built a strong ethical culture. A must-read for every would-be entrepreneur.

Sandipan Deb, *former Editor,* **The Financial Express,** *and Founder-Editor,* **Open** *and* **Swarajya** *magazines*

Saying No to Jugaad

The Making of Bigbasket: India's Biggest Online Grocery Superstore

T.N. Hari and M.S. Subramanian

BLOOMSBURY
NEW DELHI • LONDON • OXFORD • NEW YORK • SYDNEY

BLOOMSBURY INDIA
Bloomsbury Publishing India Pvt. Ltd
Second Floor, LSC Building No. 4, DDA Complex, Pocket C – 6 & 7,
Vasant Kunj New Delhi 110070

BLOOMSBURY, BLOOMSBURY INDIA and the Diana logo are trademarks of Bloomsbury Publishing Plc

First published in India 2019
This edition published in 2019

ISBN: HB: 978-93-893-5108-8; eBook: 978-93-893-5110-1

2 4 6 8 10 9 7 5 3 1

Typeset in Manipal Digital
Printed and bound in India by Thomson Press India Ltd.

No person is too small and no company too ordinary to merit a story. Everyone just needs someone who can tell their story. We were privileged to be that someone to tell the story of an extraordinary company.

I (Subramanian) would like to dedicate this book to Madhav, our little bundle of joy, who in the few hours he spent with us, taught me to lose my fears and to live in the present.

I (Hari) would like to dedicate this book to my wife Mrinalini for her unconditional support and for the sacrifices she has made for the sake of my career.

Contents

Foreword

Important principles may, and must, be inflexible.
—Abraham Lincoln

Some start-ups succeed because they are riding a wave and others because their idea or business model has caught the fancy of a few large investors. And then, there are start-ups that succeed because they are not swayed by prevailing winds and instead stick to their convictions and sound business principles.

Bigbasket is one such start-up.

Having been on the Board of Bigbasket from 2014, I have had the privilege of observing this company from close quarters. I have developed a deep respect for the way the founders have run the company and also the way they have personally evolved over the years. The quality of debate, openness to feedback and criticism and the constant pursuit of excellence stand out. My belief that energy, as well as the ability to unlearn and relearn, has little to do with age has been reinforced after seeing them in action.

The book provides a very balanced perspective of the company. It does not glorify the founders, the company or the culture. It tells the story as it is. The book is a story of the people behind the company as much as the company itself. It is full of interesting anecdotes that make for easy reading while beautifully bringing out some of the principles that went into building the company. There are lessons in this for everyone—investors, entrepreneurs and employees.

What impressed me most about Bigbasket was their ability to walk the tightrope between sticking to well-tested business principles, on the one hand, and the risk-taking needed in an era of bold bets on the other. I was also impressed with their penchant for always doing the right thing when it came to ethics and values. Often, their importance tends to get underestimated in the start-up world, but not laying the right foundation can come back to bite in a big way.

Bigbasket never forgot its identity. It was a retail company that was trying to leverage the Internet to do online commerce. It was, therefore, tech-enabled and not tech-led. This unswerving belief helped it stay the course and build the business accordingly.

Its biggest strength has been a maniacal focus on customers, and this permeated to everything it did, including how internal customers were treated by internal service providers. The chapter titled 'An Extra Pair of Shoes' brings this out clearly. There are several episodes in the book that are a true reflection of the larger customer-centric thinking in everything the company did—product quality, range, refund policies, guarantees, promotions and more. The customer is at the centre of the Bigbasket universe. In every meeting, including Board meetings, there was an imaginary pair of shoes in the room. When you spoke, you had to imagine you were standing in them. These were the shoes of the customer.

Over the years, this has led to a culture where any change that impacted a customer (be it changes in policy, levy of new fees, changes in product features or anything else) had to be preceded by a deep dive and pilots. Anyone doing anything that impacted customers was urged to see things from their perspective.

The book is partly about the celebration of achievements and partly about reflecting on the journey so far. I am yet to read a book like this that tells the story of a specific start-up so lucidly. I thoroughly enjoyed reading it. Despite being on the Board for over four years, I still found several takeaways, insights and 'aha' moments. I hope you like reading it as much as I did.

I am also delighted to introduce the authors, Hari and Subramanian. Hari has co-authored several insightful books and my association with him goes back to 2002 when we worked together at Daksh. Subramanian has studied at IIM Ahmedabad and MIT and had worked with Dell and McKinsey before joining Bigbasket. They are the best people who could have written this book, and I, on behalf of the entire Bigbasket family, am truly grateful.

—Sanjeev Aggarwal
Co-founder, Helion Ventures and Fundamentum Partnership

Acknowledgements

A book of this nature would just not have been possible without the active participation of several teams and individuals.

From the day we decided to write this book to it being available in book stores, it has been less than six months. We drove everyone crazy, including our publishers! Surprisingly, everyone, without exception, found the time to share their insights and stories despite their genuinely hectic schedules. Many of them worked weekends.

When we first spoke to the founders of Bigbasket about the idea and laid out the condition that the story had to be an honest one, they agreed instantly. They couldn't imagine it any other way. And they trusted us completely on this. In true spirit, besides providing some input and perspective, they stayed away from seeing the drafts or the final version. Nothing is more inspiring than receiving such blind trust.

We would like to thank Gopalakrishna, Vipul Mittal, Rakshit Daga, Tejas Vyas, Neelam Ahluwalia, D.V. Giri, Pooja Ravishankar and Naveen for providing input and sharing some of their stories.

Michael Fox once said, 'Family is not an important thing. It's everything.' An average professional spends 8 of his/her 16 waking hours at work and the remaining hours at home. In effect, every professional ends up having two families—one at home and one at work. These families are what keep me (Mani) grounded. I personally believe that you don't join the team—you marry into the team and they become your family at work. I have been fortunate to have my family at home to support me as I worked through the deadlines to complete the chapters in this book. To both these families, I owe my debt of gratitude.

My (Hari) daughter, who is just into the first year of college, read every single chapter enthusiastically and shared her thoughts. She didn't necessarily understand every single detail but has a refined understanding of human values and an intuition for what makes a good story. She helped smooth a few rough edges and did this very delicately. Over the years, I have learnt to take her subtle feedback seriously. Thank you, Ashu, my dearest! You will always be my top role model.

I (Hari) will always be grateful to YourStory for helping me realise that everyone has a story to tell! They just need that someone who can tell their story.

We are truly grateful to Praveen Tiwari, our publisher at Bloomsbury, who has been a constant support. It needed precisely 15 seconds for us to sell him the idea of this book. This is the kind of vote of confidence that anyone would die for. We would also like to thank Shreya Chakraborti, Editorial Manager at Bloomsbury, who was very supportive and encouraging during the whole process.

—T.N. Hari and M.S. Subramanian

1
The Dark Horse

I don't know if we each have a destiny, or if we are all just floating around accidental-like on a breeze. But I think maybe it's both.

—Forrest Gump

Following liberalisation in 1991, India enjoyed growth rates in the high single digits for several years at a stretch. The high point was when the country earned the tag of the fastest-growing large economy in 2016. Demonetisation in November 2016 temporarily displaced India from the pole position, but that did not detract from the fact that India was the new land of opportunities. It was this sudden realisation, along with the lost opportunities in China, that motivated many global venture capital (VC) firms and hedge funds to make a beeline to India and kick off a frenzy of entrepreneurial and VC activity.

Entrepreneurship in India has evolved and matured significantly since the turn of the century. Successive governments, through a combination of pragmatic policy-making and focus on execution, have accelerated this journey. The year 2018 was a high point and a culmination of several years of thoughtful and well-directed effort.

The last 10 years, particularly, have witnessed a tectonic shift in the overall start-up ecosystem. A new genre of VC-backed entrepreneurship in India had come of age. Until very recently, Indian entrepreneurs had shied away from solving local problems or working on cutting-edge technologies. One can attribute this partly to the lack of bold venture funding, as a result of which businesses had to be built around solving problems that could quickly generate positive cash flows. Many of these companies leveraged the wage arbitrage between India and the West to build companies that provided outsourced services. Companies like Infosys, Cognizant and Wipro, among others, had leveraged this opportunity to quickly grow into multi-billion dollar enterprises.

Solutions to local problems needed change in consumer behaviours and low price points. Invariably, they involved long gestation periods and cash burn. This called for investors with deep pockets, nerve and audacity. And for several reasons such investors had stayed away from India in the past.

Starting 2007, however, the trend changed and investing in start-ups that solved India's problems suddenly became attractive for VCs, given the large size of the market and the macro-story of an emerging India. Every mega trend takes concrete shape at a tipping point created by the chance confluence of several factors coupled with an avalanche of anticipation and mass exuberance. This tipping point was achieved in 2007–2008. Flipkart was at the vanguard of this revolution and the leading poster boy of this genre of entrepreneurship. Its founders inspired hundreds, if not thousands, of young Indians to take the plunge into entrepreneurship.

Some not so young second- and third-time entrepreneurs were also quick to spot the opportunities that growing Internet speed and penetration had opened up. The initial success of some of the early start-ups that leveraged this Internet revolution inspired them to take the plunge again.

This book seeks to tell the inside story of one such start-up—Bigbasket.

The founders of Bigbasket, with the sole exception of Hari Menon, are relatively low profile. Hari Menon, too, stays away from the media unless there is a material update that needs to be provided. At a personal level though, Hari Menon is a charismatic person who has interests beyond work. With his silvery white hair and an avid interest in musical numbers of the golden era—he was the lead guitarist in a rock band—he exudes an old-world charm and aura. He is also an investor in Bengaluru's lively pub, Sherlocks, where he performs occasionally. His wife Shanthi, too, is extremely talented and a high achiever. She is the principal of one of Bengaluru's leading public schools and a trained Bharatanatyam and Mohiniyattam dancer. Together, they are a high-profile power couple. Meanwhile, V.S. Sudhakar, one of the co-founders, whose stamp is imprinted on every process at Bigbasket, keeps to himself. His unwavering focus on creating excellence in every aspect of the business is as astonishing as his sense of detachment when it comes to being in the limelight. None of the founders are active on social media; most of them are not present on any platform. Only Vipul Parekh has a profile on Twitter, but his tastes are far too esoteric for most of the Twitterati—he is more interested in Richard Dawkins and Pamela Gay than Elon Musk or Donald Trump.

Initially, Bigbasket was not one of those flashy start-ups that drew attention in popular media. It was only when some of the unicorns began facing trouble because of excessive cash burn, poor unit economics and recurrent losses which were far in excess of their top-lines that Bigbasket drew attention. The way in which Bigbasket had thoughtfully managed these issues at every stage in the journey, without being influenced by practices that some of the newly-minted unicorns had popularised, began drawing grudging respect.

India was a youthful nation and pretty much everyone in the media (and most other industries) had not witnessed the hype-disappointment cycles of the past. So, it wasn't surprising that the top news and stories that the media covered was usually about funding, growth and people like themselves. Very few knew what some of the wise folks in Silicon Valley had discovered a strong and somewhat weird correlation between a start-up appearing on the cover of *Newsweek* magazine and it's almost certain near-term demise. The founders of Bigbasket had seen this cycle of hype and disappointment in the past and were victims of these themselves in their earlier entrepreneurial stint. They were, therefore, careful and wise in spending all their time in building and fine-tuning the business and staying away from media hype.

Learning to Adapt

Lessons from your past life can be helpful in navigating new terrain, but they can also constrain your thinking. Times had changed and the battleground was different. The rules of the game were being rapidly rewritten. Hedge funds from New York and Hong Kong had an audacious streak that traditional VCs, and entrepreneurs backed by these traditional VCs, had not seen before. Their bets were often, in poker terminology, the 'all in' kind. Their eyes were on changing consumer behaviour and rapidly garnering market share. They rarely asked questions on profitability or unit economics. The valuations of some of their portfolio companies had skyrocketed on the assumption that in an industry with strong network effect, there would only be one winner.

Bigbasket, too, was doing well and poised for success and, hence, had to start learning to think like a winner. It was important for the founders of Bigbasket to unlearn and relearn a few things. There was no need to swing to another extreme, but it was essential to understand the new rules of the game. And, it was quite amazing to see the grey-haired founders unlearn and relearn rapidly.

However, they never forgot some basic principles and their strengths.

Playing to Your Strengths

From time to time you need to look inside, remember who you are, always stay grounded and then decide where you want to go and how to get there!

The founders of Bigbasket had always viewed it as a 'retail' company and not a 'technology' company. In other words, technology-enabled rather than technology-led; this is a big difference. If you see yourself as a retail company, you would appreciate the importance of controlling inventory, the criticality of the supply chain, logistics, farmer tie-ups, buying and merchandising, and the part each of them plays. And each in itself is a highly evolved domain where the playbook has already been written. If you have not been part of writing this book or playing by this book, and your origins were in tech, you had to learn these domains through a combination of experimentation and imitation, neither of which is conducive for rapid scaling. If your origins were retail, you had to learn tech.

And Bigbasket chose to learn tech rapidly. In March 2012, Bigbasket brought in Pramod Jajoo, a seasoned technology professional who had worked for some of the best tech start-ups in Silicon Valley like Sun Microsystems and Healtheon, among others, as the chief technical officer (CTO).

Amazon was a great example of starting with tech and learning retail, while Walmart was an example of starting with retail and learning tech. Where one starts and what one chooses to learn depends upon one's DNA as the Yahoo example would illustrate.

Analysts have written how Yahoo never saw itself as a media company but instead as a technology and ad-serving company which eventually resulted in it fading away rather ingloriously. All this became evident post-facto. It would never have been easy for Yahoo to see itself as a media company because that was not its origins. For individuals, or companies, where you come from and who you are—your DNA essentially—matters a great deal. If your DNA fits in well with the current circumstances, you have a good chance of winning. It isn't easy to change your DNA to suit a different set of circumstances. Therefore, we've always maintained that while what got you here won't get you there has a lot of wisdom, there is also wisdom in the thought that if you forget what got you here, you may not get there! In 2015, circumstances favoured the retail DNA of Bigbasket. The great thing about Bigbasket was that it understood this well and drove home this advantage.

Founder Cohesiveness

We don't think it could get better than this. Most start-ups quickly reach a place where one (or more) of the founders is unable to add value, or is unable to cope with the rapidly changing circumstances, or is unable to manage scale, or is simply tired to play hard. On the contrary, the Bigbasket founders just seemed to get better with time. Each of them has been quite awesome at coping with change—Sudhakar is one of the sharpest minds we have ever come across. He is pretty anonymous outside of Bigbasket. No media journalist may know who he is, but his signature is there across most Bigbasket processes. He is kind of a roving consultant with primary interest in technology, product and operations. Hari Menon is the charismatic CEO who is a people person at heart and a true blue-blood retailer professionally. Co-founder Vipul Parekh is a frugal marketer and a master fundraiser. He runs two very diverse functions—Marketing and Finance. Abhinay Choudhari brings in clear thinking, a sharp understanding of different aspects of the business, a sense of humour and youthful zest. He runs the B2B business at Bigbasket. Founder V.S. Ramesh has been the sheet anchor and a steady hand. He oversees projects which include new project implementation as well as extensions to existing ones. All of them are down-to-earth, have a maniacal focus on customer experience, plenty of common sense, no respect for ceremonial stuff or fads and a lot of self-assurance. More about them later in the book.

We are generally of the belief that it is important to have one of the founders be head and shoulders above the rest and lead the way, for the most part, for a start-up to scale quickly. Even Narayana Murthy of Infosys had once made this point in an interview. Bigbasket has proved to be an exception to this conventional wisdom. A team of high-calibre individuals with complementary skills (but completely aligned on values and execution focus) can work together. And, if it works, you can achieve the kind of amplification and resonance that no single leader can hope to create.

Having said this, there is some merit in having one field commander who is in charge on a battlefield. Having several equally strong and independent-minded commanders, however well-coordinated they may be, can slow things down and come in the way of quickly marching forward. When a founder is responsible for a function, taking corrective steps when the function begins to underperform can become difficult. There was certainly a bit of all this at Bigbasket.

Can There Ever Be a Secret Sauce?

One question that some people have asked us is whether we were taking a risk by disclosing what one could claim as Bigbasket's IP or secret sauce. We are confident that competitive advantage is mostly inimitable. If anyone believes that one could imitate and get ahead by reading about what others have done, they must be kidding themselves. The advantage or edge is never about an idea, a policy or a process. It is always in the intangible stuff like collaboration, teamwork, quality of execution, passion and values that all go into making the idea, the policy or process work on the ground every day. How can anyone replicate this?

Everyone Is like a 'Box of Chocolates'

Every company is unique in its own way and Bigbasket is no different. There are elements of the Bigbasket identity and signature that give it an edge, while there are other elements that have been a bit of a drag. This book is a balanced biography of Bigbasket and is not intended to be a panegyric of either the company or the people involved. It is a real story about real events and real people. It is a showcase of grit and tenacity without attempting to hide any of the imperfections and warts. It is as much about the journey as it is about the people who were a part of this journey. Between the two of us, we have over seven years of work experience at Bigbasket and our views have crystallised over these years. They are entirely our own.

In a few cases where it was important to keep the identities of the individuals confidential, we have changed their names and a few other specifics. Every incident, story and interaction we have described is true to the facts and is an accurate portrayal. We have used both 'I' and 'We' in the narration depending upon whether one or both of us together had shared an experience.

Saying No to Jugaad

Jugaad is a good strategy for innovation when resources are a constraint. Frugal innovation is often dubbed as jugaad in the Indian context. When demystified, jugaad is about using band-aids to solve a problem in the short term but often leaving the root cause unaddressed. It is perfectly all right if one is aware that she is using a band-aid because of either resource or time constraints. The problem is when this awareness is missing. This results in a culture where quick resolutions rather than long-term fixes become the norm.

Jugaad is not an Indian invention. When time and resources are a constraint, everyone, everywhere in the world, has resorted to it. Bigbasket, too, adopted jugaad and used band-aid solutions. But, the default approach was to always get to the root of an issue and fix it. However, in specific situations where 'speed to market' was critical, jugaad was inevitable. The tech debt that was created in the early days was enormous, but everyone was aware of this. This had to be cleaned up some day and this cleaning up had to come at a cost. But, there was no choice.

The journey has not been very smooth or the success unqualified. There were several obstacles and potholes along the way. But, every obstacle was an opportunity for learning and we look back at every step of the journey with pride!

We hope you like reading this as much as we liked putting this together. We also sincerely hope that in this story of Bigbasket, there is broader learning and inspiration for anyone reading this. If you can have even a few 'aha' or wow moments, our objective behind putting this together would have been accomplished.

2
Of Genes and Memes

Apart from values and ethics which I have tried to live by, the legacy I would like to leave behind is a very simple one—that I have always stood up for what I consider to be the right thing, and I have tried to be as fair and equitable as I could be.

—Ratan Tata

Sometime in September 2015, Hari Menon, Sudhakar and I (Hari) were on the same flight and had a wait time of two hours at the Shamshabad airport in Hyderabad. We chatted about several things, but the topic that stuck in my mind was about the Bigbasket culture. The Board had given the go-ahead to expand rapidly into 17 carefully selected tier 2 cities along with Kolkata and Ahmedabad. We were also in negotiations to acquire Delyver, India's first hyper-local start-up. It was evident that we would soon be: a) going on a hiring spree and b) integrating companies that Bigbasket would be acquiring.

Rapid Scaling Can Tear Apart the Culture

The biggest problem with rapid scaling has always been about being able to preserve some of the core values and culture.

We took a call to explicitly define the elements of our culture, create a code of conduct and communicate these widely. Every employee had to read and sign off on the code of conduct. We began using every forum and every leadership meet to reinforce these, and holding everyone accountable for these values. Senior leaders had to demonstrate their commitment to these values by living them every day. Nobody cares about what you say, but everyone cares about what you do.

One of the debates we had while defining the elements of Bigbasket's culture was whether they should reflect the current reality of who we are in its entirety, or did it make sense to build a small aspiration component of what we would like to be. We decided to use a 3:1 ratio—75 per cent to reflect who we really are currently and 25 per cent to reflect what we wanted to learn and imbibe. For instance, Bigbasket was not particularly known for 'speed' or 'agility', but we believed it was important. So we called out a culture element, 'Speed and a sense of urgency in everything we do.' This was one of the four elements of the culture we articulated. The other three truly reflected what we already did well: 'A maniacal focus on customers', 'Ownership even if everything is not in your control' and 'Freedom, but personal responsibility for doing the right thing'.

Putting Your Money Where Your Mouth Is

On a late Wednesday evening, in October 2016, Tanuja Tewari, the no-nonsense HR head at Bigbasket, received a call from Stephanie Paul, the person in charge of HR Audit and Compliance. Tanuja was providing directions to her Uber cab driver when Stephanie called. After she boarded the cab, she called Stephanie back. When she heard what Stephanie had to say, she was livid.

During the audit of one of the regions, a woman in the regional HR team had started crying. When probed, she hesitatingly disclosed that she was being sexually harassed by the regional HR head, Praveen Mhatre. She was the sole breadwinner in her family and was afraid she would lose her job if she complained. Stephanie was surprised. As she probed a little deeper, she was told that Praveen had been sexually harassing other women in the team as well. Stephanie immediately did her own quick investigation by talking to all the women in the team. She gathered the preliminary evidence in the form of statements as well as messages on WhatsApp before calling Tanuja.

Bigbasket had put in place a well-thought-out policy on Prevention of Sexual Harassment (POSH) in 2016. The policy was crafted and communicated with the serious intent of creating a truly safe and harassment-free workplace for its entire staff.

Bigbasket employed a wide variety of women. There were smart and educated women in corporate teams who were well aware of their rights and the recourse they had if these were violated. In the warehouses, which were scattered throughout the country, there was a second category of women employees. They were part of the blue-collar workforce and were often the sole breadwinners in their families. Their formative years had not instilled in them the necessary strength and courage to ward off harassment by men in positions of authority. Tanuja was fully aware of this and wanted a policy that would guarantee the safety and security of such women who were in far-flung locations, outside the scrutiny and protective umbrella of the corporate life. While a thoughtful policy was important, she realised that it was the flawless implementation on the ground, in every one of the hundreds of warehouses, stores, collection centres and trans-shipment sites, that finally mattered.

Tanuja had also brought in Shubha Chacko, a woman who had built a reputation in handling a variety of issues related to women's safety and welfare as an advisor. Shubha had played an important role in shaping

Bigbasket's POSH policy. She also participated in all the investigations. Having a strong external member sit in on the investigations would ensure that the process was transparent and not susceptible to any kind of undue influence as well as help overcome some blind spots and unconscious biases that were bound to play out when viewed by an insider. While the probability of any undue influence at Bigbasket was very low, it was important to ensure that prevention and redressal mechanisms were foolproof and did not just rely on the good intentions of the leadership team. 'Trust in God but lock your car' was Tanuja's motto. Who could say when the devil would possess someone!

After the POSH policy was put in place, this was the first case of a complaint. Ironically, the accused was someone who was the custodian and protector of the policy. Praveen was well connected in the local labour unions and moved around in small-time political circles in the city. The city was a difficult place to do business in and one needed to know how to navigate the knotty web of labour unions, local mafia and political patronage if your business was to survive and thrive. Praveen was seen by everyone as indispensable if Bigbasket had to do business in this city. This may not have been as much about Praveen's grasp of the local politics as much as an indication of how little the rest of the company, especially those working in the corporate set-up, understood about the murky side of doing business in a politically volatile environment.

Internal stakeholders were not particularly happy with Praveen's performance and employee centricity, but they were somewhat helpless because of his supposed understanding of the local dynamics.

The complaint was grave. A formal and thorough investigation was launched immediately. The Internal

Complaints Committee (ICC) convened several times over the next 48 hours, listened to all the parties, examined all the evidence and submitted its report. The recommendation was to terminate Praveen's employment. The ICC at Bigbasket had been constituted very thoughtfully and members were drawn from both the regional and corporate offices to ensure that no complaint could ever be hushed up.

Tanuja had made up her mind to take the bull by the horns and deal with any fallout of his termination. The ICC had made its recommendation on Friday evening. She was in agreement with the recommendation and sought approval for Praveen's termination from Sudhakar and Hari Menon the same night. The next morning she called up Sudhakar and Hari Menon to discuss this and had secured their approval to execute the ICC's decision. She told me several months later that while she had no doubt that the management would go with the ICC recommendation, in the remote case of them dragging their feet, she was prepared to quit. Over the following months and years, she would learn that when it came to ethics or values, the Bigbasket management team rarely dragged their feet.

Stephanie was asked to extend her stay. Tanuja called up the region business head, Sreedhar, and apprised him of the developments. He had not been informed about the inquiry process. The process did not require him to be kept in the loop. Sreedhar was worried about the fallout. Tanuja assured him complete support until a replacement was found and explained that it was important to do the right thing. She did not believe in displaying the iron fist behind the velvet glove when the velvet glove was enough to persuade someone to do the right thing. Fortunately, Sreedhar quickly understood and agreed on the line of action. Praveen was called to Sreedhar's office. Tanuja was on call from Bengaluru, while Stephanie and Sreedhar were present in person. The decision was communicated to Praveen. Praveen seemed like he had been anticipating this since he had appeared before the ICC, but had been hopeful that he would be let off with a stern warning. He had misjudged Bigbasket's resolve.

This incident is a reflection on the broader approach to handling matters related to any violations of the code of conduct.

Through intense communication and education, the consequences of any violation of the POSH policy had been disseminated widely. Understanding something as complex as to why someone would violate a policy like this, despite fully knowing the consequences, would be a psychologist's delight. While this didn't seem enough to deter everyone, redressal has always been swift, and the long arm of the company law has always caught up with the offenders irrespective of their position in the organisation and their seeming indispensability—every single time.

The commitment to doing the right thing ran deep. When I (Hari) came on board in March 2015, I noticed that the employee stock option plans were quite one-sided (in favour of the company). It was obvious that they were structured by lawyers and the founders had not realised the full import of some of the clauses. The founders and the Board were quick to appreciate the implications once explained and revisions were signed off. Within a week, all the earlier agreements that employees had signed were replaced by new ones that incorporated the revisions.

It was the same when it came to treating vendors and other partners. Fairness was what mattered.

People Believe What You Do and Not What You Say

Every April, we have an annual function to celebrate the best of the previous year. A glittering reward and recognition ceremony is a part of this function. The Management Council would discuss all nominations. When the Management Council met in April 2018 to discuss the nominations, and the discussion moved to the Bigbasket 'Beacon of Values' award, it became evident that Stephanie Paul's name bubbled up to the top. She had won the award last year and the year before as well. So, the question was whether we should consider someone else this year. Finally, the consensus was to award her the winning trophy again!

Stephanie grew up in an Anglo-Indian family in a very small town, about 100 kilometres from Bengaluru, where her mother taught English in a primary school. Her mother was the sole earner in the family and a big influence on her life. From her mother, she had learnt the importance of always doing the right thing. At the award ceremony, this is what she had to say, 'My belief is that all that we go through in this journey of life will connect eventually. God is always there to show us the way. I care about honesty, respect and loyalty. My mother was the biggest influence in my life. She was a very kind woman, worked hard for the family with no complaints, and her selflessness touched me deeply.'

Stephanie had lost her mother under very tragic circumstances. Processing payroll at Bigbasket was complex because of the different types of associates (on-roll/off-roll/micro-entrepreneurs), the sheer numbers, attendance validation, overtime computation, the geographical spread and the complex incentive structures. When it was payroll time, she worked like a person possessed to ensure an error-free payroll. She deeply cared for the employees, especially the blue-collar staff, and ensured that everyone was paid correctly every time. It was distressing to later know that Stephanie was with her laptop in the hospital on that unfortunate day. Unknown to anyone, she was keeping a tab on the payroll process when her mother was in her final moments before death. It was heartbreaking to imagine her drawing a balance between employees who were dear to her and her mother who was personally dearest to her.

This decision to award Stephanie for the third year in a row reflected a broader philosophy—rewards were not going to be by rotation. The best will always win. We realised that once we go down the path of rotating rewards, the teams would lose faith in the value of these awards, and irrespective of what we said about the best talent being recognised, no one would trust us ever. One wrong act could neutralise a hundred statements of good intent. As someone said, one teaching moment leveraged well is more powerful than a thousand CEO speeches.

Frugality or Penny-Pinching?

Bigbasket was known for being a frugal organisation. In March 2015 when I (Hari) came on board, a few things surprised me based on what I had experienced at three of my last high-growth start-ups.

Bigbasket was structured as regional business units (RBUs). Each RBU was reasonably self-sufficient and most corporate functions were replicated in the unit. This was the right structure for a company poised for growth. However, there were some very visible exceptions and flaws. Unlike the rest of the regions, the biggest RBU of Bengaluru did not have an RBU head (RBH); nor did it have a head of HR. The logic was that since the company was headquartered in Bengaluru, the corporate team would somehow run the RBU. Of course, no one at the corporate either had the time to run it nor was it a part of anyone's objectives and key results. The company was avoiding a small cost by not staffing these roles. However, everyday conflicts, friction and process deviations that needed an RBH to intervene were festering. The day-to-day coordination between the different function heads in the region was broke, as a result of which decisions were not taken on time and key issues remained unresolved. The basic HR processes around attendance, payroll, compliance and employee welfare weren't in place. Salaries were being paid without a robust attendance management system and sometimes to people who were no longer employed with the company. In an instant, I (Hari) could sense that the cost avoided by not having a business and human resources head was a fraction of the intangible (and tangible) damage created by not having these two roles staffed.

Similarly, Pune, which was becoming an important region and had tremendous growth potential, was overseen by the Mumbai RBH on a part-time basis. This was neither good for Mumbai nor for Pune.

There were other key functions that were being managed for far too long with undersized individuals creating breakages and stakeholder dissatisfaction. Some examples were IT Infra, Marketing and Product, among others. Building a consensus with so many founders was not easy. A clear reporting structure and unambiguous decision-making process would have solved many of these problems. Even as 2018 came to an end, a company of Bigbasket's size, complexity and sensitivities did not have a General Counsel. The risk was high. Hari Menon had already been summoned by a sessions court in Mumbai for something that was totally avoidable.

In each of these cases, the problem was the same, that is, the inability to easily distinguish between a bad cost and a good cost; the inability to fully appreciate the extent of leakage or lost opportunity caused by not incurring a good cost on time.

These were some of the discussions I had with Hari Menon and Sudhakar during my early days at Bigbasket.

They understood this but still didn't seem to believe that these needed to be fixed on a war footing. To their credit, they did figure these out soon and eventually all of these gaps were addressed, some sooner than the rest.

I soon realised that even the best people have their blind spots, and to understand why someone operates with these blind spots or behaves in a particular way, you need to know their history a little bit.

Marshall Goldsmith had once observed, 'What got you here won't get you there.' A very powerful quote in a specific context, the counter to this is that if you forget who you are, where you come from and what got you here, you certainly won't get where you intend to go.

The true essence of the Bigbasket story is that the founders never forgot the lessons from their last venture, Fabmart.

There, the founders had realised that it is easy to spend money and build large teams, but it is not easy to run a business with thin margins profitably. Some of these lessons had been etched deeply into their DNA. The years 2014 and 2015 witnessed mindless cash burn and a collective loss of rational thinking in the start-up community in India. This reminded us of the heady days that led up to the subprime crisis. It is easy to be carried away by such a tidal wave. It needs some nerve to stand up to this and stick to reason.

Grocery retail is a low-margin business. Therefore, avoiding costs and conservatism had been drilled into their thinking. In the process, they took some right calls that stood the test of time. Walk into any of Bigbasket's head offices in Bengaluru and you will get a good sense of the frugal culture. The approach it has taken to recruiting talent, the kind of teams it had built, the timing of key recruits and the facilities it works from are a clear testimony to a well-run business.

Their excessive focus on cost avoidance also made them take some wrong calls, some of which we discussed earlier.

In balance, we have no doubt that there were more right calls than wrong ones.

Punching Above Your Weight Class

When I (Hari) joined Bigbasket in March 2015, Hari Menon had taken me around the country, introducing me to all the teams in the regions. Bigbasket was then a far smaller company in terms of geographical spread than it is now, and could afford the luxury of this kind of an induction. In the process, I was also introduced to all the corporate function heads. When I was introduced to Gopala Krishna (fondly referred to as Gopala), who was the national head of Warehousing and Supply Chain at the corporate office in Bengaluru, Hari Menon could not help noticing the surprise on my face. He took me aside and whispered, 'Don't go by his English.'

It took me a while to figure out the merit behind this seemingly strange choice.

Gopala grew up in a nondescript village in Andhra Pradesh. His parents had a three-acre farm that was given out for cultivation to another family. The deal was that Gopala's family would get half of whatever the farm produced. His father had tried his hand at various small jobs but nothing worked out. The atmosphere at home was not the best for children. Surprisingly, this did not seem to have had an impact on Gopala's adult life. His calmness and an ever-smiling face, which is on display even during the most stressful of situations, hides the traumas he had to go through in his younger days. He carries no bitterness. His father now lives with him.

After graduating from high school, Gopala went to Machilipatnam, the nearest provincial town, for further studies. His medium of education, until he went to college, was Telugu. English as a language was part of his syllabus, but he barely managed to pass this subject every year. In the final year of high school, he secured only 36 per cent in English. His struggle with English still continues.

After graduating in commerce, his mother reached out to a close relative in Hyderabad to help her son get employment. The relative took him to a few places. Gopala finally took up a job at a small workshop that did contract manufacturing for a factory nearby. Gopala's job was to go to the factory every week and collect orders. When the order was fulfilled, he had to deliver the machined components to the factory.

He did this for a while until he found another job at a third-party logistics firm where he had to keep a record of the utilisation of the 'way bills'. A way bill is a document issued by a carrier giving details and instructions relating to the shipment of a consignment of goods. The records were manually maintained. One evening, instead of going home, he sat at the only personal computer in the office and transcribed all the records into an Excel sheet. When he showed a neat printout of the records to his manager, he was unimpressed. 'The sales tax authority won't accept anything other than the handwritten version,' he was told. Gopala offered to meet the sales tax inspector and understand what exactly the issue was. The inspector didn't seem to have a problem with the printed records and starting that day, the process of managing the 'way bills' was automated.

This streak of improving processes has continued till this day.

Gopala took on a mortgage, bought a house and settled his family in Machilipatnam. His mother along with a couple of her grandchildren still stays in this home. He has two sisters, one elder to him and the other younger. He took personal responsibility for getting his younger sister married—from finding the groom to organising the wedding.

After some more jobs, he was interviewed at Bigbasket. He had been referred to Bigbasket by an old acquaintance, Hari Krishna Reddy, who had just moved to the company. The three founders offered him a job the same day. He joined Bigbasket on 3 December 2012 and hasn't looked back since.

He speaks reasonably well English now, though his written communication is still a bit of a challenge. I've always maintained that what differentiates start-ups from more mature firms is the importance of substance over style. Gopala is a living example of that.

Bigbasket believed in hiring and grooming people who could punch above their weight. While a lot of the contemporary start-ups chose to bet on high-education pedigree and recruited from premium engineering and business schools, Bigbasket decided to go down a different path. Many of the early employees came with very modest qualifications.

Ivy League education often comes at a disproportionate premium. Even when Bigbasket picked people from top colleges and universities, it was only after they cleared an attitude fit. The two components of attitude fit were an ability to work with others who didn't have access to a privileged education and not creating internal cliques.

As Bigbasket scaled, it brought in people for key functions with premium education along with ground-up problem-solving skills. Obviously, they had to pass the attitude test. Once in a while though, the thought did occur to me (Hari) that we may have missed accelerating our journey because of the reluctance to bring in some of these laterals a little earlier in the journey.

An amazing component of Bigbasket's culture was that employees with a pedigreed education assimilated well with internal stars. A big problem with a lot of rapidly growing start-ups is the inevitable conflict between the lateral hires and the internal stars who had built their reputation and relationship with the founding team. Laterals were hired very thoughtfully. An ability to drive a trajectory change in their existing domain was important, but the ability to work with humility was equally necessary.

Aggression is not a part of the broader culture at Bigbasket. Differences and conflicts are rarely vocal and sometimes issues are not directly addressed. The founders did not hesitate to ask difficult questions, but, if measured across the board, it was a relatively soft culture. Non-performers would be given coaching and a chance to show improvement. Sometimes, there were too many chances. People who were loyal were allowed to continue for far too long in roles that had outgrown them, with the argument that it was the role of leaders to groom and support these individuals in scaling their abilities. The broader belief was that while aggression was important, control was the key.

Competitors Are Not Enemies

We were building our meats business and interviewing candidates who could fit this role. During the course of one such interview, the candidate began disclosing specific elements of strategy along with revenue numbers of his current company. Seshu Kumar, who is our buying and merchandising head, interrupted the candidate and told him that this was neither necessary nor right. The candidate was dropped.

While competition is inevitable, it is important where you draw the line. We have always strongly discouraged people we hire from bringing any kind of documents or presentations from their previous organisations. We are also very reluctant to hire people who bad-mouth their current or any of their previous organisations, even if it happened to be a competitor. We don't believe that you have to bad-mouth a competitor to demonstrate your love for Bigbasket. On the contrary, we see it as a sign of immaturity.

From time to time, some of the smaller start-ups in the same industry as Bigbasket would reach out to founders and other members of the management team for direction and guidance, and it was considered perfectly all right to give them advice. One of Bigbasket's core values was 'Freedom but Personal Responsibility in Everything' and it was expected that everyone in the leadership team knew where to draw the line in such a scenario. When some of the competitors had to shut, Bigbasket worked very closely with their leadership team in helping them outplace their employees who were laid off.

Calm and Self-Assured

This story would reveal a very important strength of Bigbasket.

It was an overcast sky during the monsoon of 2015 and there was a slight drizzle—typical Bengaluru weather from May through September. Hari Menon and Vipul Parekh were huddled in a cramped conference room at Bigbasket's unpretentious and spartan head office in the tree-lined suburb of Indiranagar. Lee Fixel of Tiger Global was coming to meet them in five minutes.

Tiger Global was a New York-based hedge fund. Hedge funds had traditionally operated in the public markets domain, and kind of guaranteed an above market rate of return by deploying sophisticated hedging strategies. Starting in 2008, through quantitative easing and a set of other measures, the Federal Reserve Bank of New York had brought down the interest rate to near zero and funds of all kinds (hedge funds, pension funds, university endowments) were scouting for avenues with better returns and began seriously considering venture investment as an asset class.

Lee Fixel, a partner at Tiger Global, had rapidly emerged as the demigod of the nascent Indian e-commerce sector. He had made several bold bets and was touted to have the Midas touch. His combined investment in Flipkart, Ola, Delhivery, Quickr and Shopclues was in excess of $1.5 billion. In May 2018, *Mint* reported that in Walmart's acquisition of Flipkart, Lee could end up making more than $3.5 billion for Tiger Global on an investment of less than $1 billion and still retain a 4–5 per cent stake in Flipkart. This changed the narrative in an exit-starved market.

When Lee and Tiger Global invested in a start-up, it was a big moral—and often real—setback for every other competitor in the space. Tiger Global's bold betting strategy, deep pockets and their ability to persuade other deep-pocketed investors to participate in the subsequent rounds of funding had become legendary. Businesses that needed sustained cash for scaling could not afford to have Tiger Global in the rival camp. Tiger Global was now scouting for a grocery e-commerce start-up to invest in.

Bigbasket's founders were aware of this and were keenly awaiting the meeting with Lee to see how the conversation would go.

Lee and Kalyan Krishnamurthy, who was then a partner at Tiger Global, were on time for the meeting. The meeting lasted for 30 minutes.

Five minutes into the meeting and it was evident that Bigbasket's asset-heavy model didn't appeal to the duo. At the end of the meeting, Lee and Kalyan communicated in a very oblique way that the new asset-light models, which made a lot of sense from a scaling perspective, would prevail. The implicit message was, 'You guys are likely to see competition in this space, and you better watch out.' There was also a strong industry buzz that Tiger Global backed only young founders. By that yardstick, the Bigbasket founders were too old for them.

Soon, Tiger Global announced an investment in Grofers. Softbank soon followed Tiger. Sequoia was already an early investor in Grofers. The three were a formidable alliance and this was not the first time they had come together to back a company.

Every start-up that attempted online grocery delivery in an asset-light model either pivoted to an inventory model or shut shop. For a short while, all of them had scaled rapidly but the bad customer experience they created was their ultimate undoing. You couldn't rely on delivery boys picking up fruits and vegetables for customers from the nearest stores and doing a good job of it. Besides, stores in India were a long way from sharing their inventory with online grocery companies on a real-time basis. As a result, the online company that fulfilled a customer order had no clue as to how many items in the order they could fulfil and hence had to accept orders blindly. And finally, they delivered only a part of the order and forced the customer to visit an offline store for the balance items. The customer may have as well bought the entire basket from the offline store. And ironically, the value proposition that an online provider offered was that you needn't visit an offline store.

Like most grocery start-ups that began with an asset-light model, Flipkart's initial foray, under the brand name Nearby, was short-lived. When Flipkart re-launched grocery for the second time, which they did with an inventory model, Nishant Sharma wrote an article in *Bloomberg Quint* (11 August 2018) titled, 'Flipkart founder's first grocery hurdle is to wean away wife from Bigbasket'. In it, he wrote, 'For Flipkart group co-founder and chief executive officer Binny Bansal, the challenge to crack the grocery market starts at home.' He quotes Binny Bansal, 'My wife is a Bigbasket customer and I'm trying to convince her to buy groceries from Flipkart.'

The Galileo Moment

Tiger Global's decision, followed quickly by Softbank, to back a rival model was one of the toughest moments for the Bigbasket founders. It tested their resolve and self-confidence. They had a choice to defer to the popes of the investing world, change their position and accept that the sun went round the Earth or stick to what they knew for sure—that an asset-light model would never work for grocery in India.

A Board meeting was soon convened to evaluate the implications of this development. The founders stuck to their guns and explained their logic once again to the Board. The Board needed this reassurance and solidly backed the founders.

There was one change that Bigbasket had been contemplating making and Tiger Global's decision accelerated that change. Bigbasket had realised quite early that in India 70–75 per cent of grocery purchase was planned at the beginning of the month. Around 20 per cent was top-up purchases mid-month or mid-week. And 5 per cent of the purchases were from local specialty stores. Bigbasket had been servicing the planned monthly purchase and had been contemplating catering to the top-up requirements through an express service. And that is how Bigbasket ended up acquiring Delyver. This story is covered in greater detail in the chapter titled 'Thoughtful about Build or Buy'.

The biggest turning point in Bigbasket's journey was in sticking to what they knew worked well despite two of the biggest investors backing a rival model.

In Conclusion

Explaining the importance of culture is a difficult task. Everyone has heard of culture and values, but very few truly understand how they impact business. And this ignorance is not limited to only those new to corporate life. Those with decades of experience are often exactly in the same boat when it came to understanding what culture really is, how it could impact business or how they could directly influence it. Unless this was demystified, anything we did around culture would be a waste of time. And Bigbasket didn't believe in doing anything as a ritual, unless it had tangible outcomes.

So, we used game theory and the power of the ubiquitous 2 by 2 matrix to explain culture. We took the fluff out of culture and explained it in a language that professionals brought up on a strong diet of logic could relate to. We came up with several examples, including clips from popular Bollywood and Hollywood films, to drive a series of conversations across the company. We ensured that the senior leadership in every function and every region understood the culture model. A big lesson was that if the senior leadership understands how culture can drive business, the results are magical.

Culture is really a collection of interrelated memes. The dictionary definition of a meme is: 'An element of a culture or system of behaviour passed from one individual to another by imitation or other non-genetic means.' Memes get disseminated if influencers and leaders start living these elements and speak about them often.

And finally, no culture is good or bad. It is what it is. Culture is who you are. Just as individuals can learn along the way but cannot easily change who they truly are, companies, too, can learn and adapt but will find it difficult to be very different from what they deeply are.

Some years later, in one of my conversations with Kabeer Biswas, the founder of the much-adored start-up Dunzo, he articulated a concern, 'How do you preserve empathy for customers and partners (Dunzo's core value was 'empathy') as Dunzo scales?' For Dunzo, it may have been empathy they wanted to preserve and for some other start-up, it could be something different. At least 20 other start-ups that had crossed the product-market fit and gone into scaling mode have asked me (Hari) the same question. Even founders with a hardcore tech background who may have never cared about this, suddenly seem to figure out that as their start-ups scaled, preserving the cool culture they had created would be their biggest challenge.

Fortunately, I (Hari) had given this subject a lot of thought and had gone through this journey several times over to have a meaningful conversation every time this question came up.

3

An Extra Pair of Shoes

There is only one boss. The customer. And he can fire everybody in the company from the chairman on down, simply by spending his money somewhere else!

—Sam Walton

Abhinay Choudhari grew up in Bhopal, the capital of Madhya Pradesh. His father worked at Bharat Heavy Electricals Limited, one of India's premier public sector undertakings (PSUs). India's PSU townships were some of the best places for children to grow up in—company-run schools that were highly subsidised, large playgrounds, lazy Sunday mornings, neatly laid-out neighbourhoods, along with a cosmopolitan and liberal culture. One got to celebrate India's incredible diversity and experience the common threads that held the seemingly diverse elements in one piece. No wonder India has been referred to at different times as a subcontinent and a salad bowl.

Abhinay was in the ninth grade when his elder sister, Anita, opened a small store that sold ready-made garments. As a young boy, every evening after school, Abhinay would visit his sister's store. He would observe customers and interact with them. Slowly he got a sense of what they were looking for and how to drive sales. After some months, he began accompanying his brother Anil to places like Delhi, Mumbai and Ahmedabad for buying garments from the wholesale markets. Little did he know that this ongoing lesson of over 10 years would be priceless when he would start his own company many years later.

In 1999, like many others, Abhinay too was attracted by the possibilities of online commerce and launched his first start-up, Style Country (a one-stop destination for branded lifestyle products like apparel, accessories, etc.). He tried to replicate the customer experience of his sister's store through a pop-up that would detail textures for apparel fabrics and an online trial room to match shirts/tops with trousers/bottoms). He tied up with India's top 35 brands and with Gati, then a leading logistics company that specialised in express delivery, to distribute his products across a thousand cities. Citibank provided the payment gateway.

Everything was going well until the dotcom market crashed and wiped out anyone who was a part of this.

In June 1999, K. Vaitheeswaran along with V.S. Sudhakar, Vipul Parekh, Hari Menon, V.S. Ramesh and Sundeep Thakran founded India's first e-commerce company, Fabmart. Fabmart was officially launched in September 1999. It began by offering only music CDs for sale. Between February and October 2000, the website introduced additional categories, such as books, movies, watches and grocery. In February 2002, the venture also built a physical retail chain called Fabmall, which was later acquired by the Aditya Birla Group and rebranded as 'More'. One couldn't miss the irony when 'More' itself was acquired by Amazon last year. Bigbasket would eventually be pitted against Amazon in a new round of bloody war for supremacy in grocery and one of Amazon's weapons in this battle would be an asset that the founders of Bigbasket had built in their previous avatar.

Vaitheeswaran carried forward the online venture under a new name, Indiaplaza.com. V.S. Sudhakar, Vipul Parekh,

Hari Menon and V.S. Ramesh went their different ways before again coming together with Abhinay Choudhari to launch Bigbasket.

But despite being the first mover, Indiaplaza could not deal with the aggression of new players like Flipkart and Snapdeal and had to shut in 2013. Incidentally, Vaitheeswaran went on to write a book, *Failing to Succeed*, where he cautioned entrepreneurs about the dark side of starting up. He would be happy that this book tells the story of a successful start-up that his co-founders at Fabmart went on to build in their next avatar.

Abhinay got in touch with the founders of Fabmart (the other four founders of Bigbasket were then running Fabmart) to see if Style Country could merge with it. Fabmart was struggling with its own set of challenges at that time and the merger talks never progressed. Style Country had to be shut down.

It was back to a corporate job for Abhinay, but the entrepreneur in him never gave up. While he was at the London office of Infosys Consulting, he experienced the convenience of buying grocery online and felt India needed this service. It was his eureka moment.

Having shopped for grocery in places as diverse as Bhopal's weekly markets to London, Toronto, Las Vegas and Bengaluru, Abhinay was quick to realise that unless you could help a customer avoid a trip to the store, the idea wouldn't take off. He pledged his savings of nearly $400,000 and started his next venture, ShopasULike. After some conversations, METRO Cash & Carry, an international self-service wholesaler, agreed to partner with him. For the first time ever, METRO Cash & Carry had agreed to share its data on inventory with a partner. This was a coup of sorts for ShopasULike. Given the limitation of funds, Abhinay chose to start with an asset-light model by not carrying any inventory. As soon as the back-end integration with METRO was complete, he launched his online platform in April 2010.

At this time, a former boss and mentor from the IT services company IGATE, Kanth Miriyala, advised Abhinay to start identifying co-founders.

After the sale of Fabmall, V.S. Sudhakar, Vipul Parekh, Hari Menon and V.S. Ramesh had decided to try out new things. Among other things, they had also signed up as advisors to ShopasULike in July 2010. ShopasULike kept scaling and adding more residential complexes in Bengaluru for home delivery of grocery. In July 2011, three promoter groups—Ganesh, Meena and Srinivas Anumolu; the Fab (Fabmart) four; and Abhinay Choudhari—came together. In October, these three groups decided to marshal all their resources and launch a new company and brand.

And that was how Bigbasket was born on 3 December 2011 as a pan-Bengaluru service. All customers from ShopasULike migrated to the new platform that night. Bigbasket quickly expanded to Mumbai and Hyderabad. The common factor was that METRO Cash & Carry had a strong presence in both these cities.

Lessons from Webvan: The Grocery Start-up that Failed Big

Webvan was an online grocery start-up in the US funded by the likes of Sequoia, Benchmark Capital, Softbank and Goldman Sachs. At its November 1999 blockbuster IPO, Webvan raised $375 million and the company was valued at $1.2 billion. However, very soon it began running huge losses, estimated at more than $800 million and filed for bankruptcy.

There were some very important lessons to be learnt from Webvan's failure:

- Webvan was founded by Louis Borders, who had no experience in the retail sector. It hired George Shaheen as a professional CEO. Shaheen was previously the CEO of Andersen Consulting who had no operational background in retail. And finally as the losses mounted, Shaheen was replaced by Robert Swan from General Electric who too had no experience in the grocery or supermarket business.
- Webvan had expanded rapidly to new markets without demonstrating operational viability or product-market fit in their first market in the San Francisco Bay Area.
- Webvan splurged on infrastructure and signed up global engineering giant Bechtel to help create state-of-the-art order fulfillment centres with robots. Each of these fulfillment centres was built at a cost of $30 million. While these centres received a lot of PR, they were inherently too sophisticated to make sense in a low-margin grocery business.

Bigbasket had understood each of these three lessons deeply from day one.

After Webvan filed for bankruptcy, Mike Moritz, who represented Sequoia on the Board, was eloquent about Webvan's reasons for failure. It is a different matter that even after this, Sequoia never seemed to get its e-commerce bets in India right.

Standing in the Customer's Shoes

Online grocery companies that started before and after Bigbasket had made the easy choice of sticking to dry grocery. Customers were shopping online so that they could avoid a trip to the store. And this visit to the store could be avoided only if the online grocer could supply their entire basket. If customers had to visit the supermarket to buy chilled and frozen items or, for that matter, fresh vegetables and fruits, they might as well shop for everything at offline stores.

The reason that no online grocery start-up had dared to enter these categories was simple—the supply chains for these categories were almost impossible to create.

The second reason customers stayed away from most online grocery stores was that companies had ignored the issue of 'fill rate'. Unless you knew about the retail industry, you didn't appreciate how important the fill rate was. Delivering a high fill rate is extremely difficult. Fill rate is a measure of the extent to which a customer order is fulfilled. For instance, if a customer ordered 20 items and you delivered 15 items, the fill rate was 75 per cent. A good fill rate, averaging across all customers, that would create customer delight, had to be 99.5 per cent or more. This called for a deep understanding of inventory management, forecasting techniques, limitations and capabilities of the supply chain, and behaviours of large distributors and manufacturers.

Customers were also disappointed by unscheduled deliveries. They preferred a specific and pre-defined slot for delivery, a slot that the customer could choose at the time of placing the order. This was again a difficult logistics problem to solve. TESCO had done this in the UK. From day one, Bigbasket decided to deliver in slots that customers had picked when they placed their orders.

Right from the beginning, Bigbasket had looked at everything from a customer's perspective. In every meeting there was an imaginary pair of shoes in the room. When you spoke, you had to imagine you were standing in them. These were the shoes of the customer.

This resulted in numbers no other online grocery company had managed to achieve. Bigbasket registered a near 100 per cent fill rate from day one. It delivered fruits and vegetables as well as chilled and frozen items from day one. It also introduced 100 per cent slotted delivery from day one. Bigbasket understood that if they couldn't maintain these numbers, it would soon end up as an undifferentiated 'me too' service. But, if it cracked these three problems, it would be untouchable.

During the early days of Bigbasket, METRO delivered a fill rate of nearly 85 per cent. After the picking was complete at the METRO store, a message would be relayed for the balance 15 per cent to pickers stationed at Hypercity. Even after picking at Hypercity, 5 per cent of the customer basket remained unfulfilled and this would be relayed to pickers stationed at select stores near the hub.

All the items were finally assembled at the space that Safal had provided to Bigbasket adjacent to their store at Whitefield, a Bengaluru suburb that was the epicentre of Bigbasket's customer base. This was Bigbasket's first customer hub. Safal was a large private wholesale company that dealt in fruits and vegetables. And, the fruits and vegetables that were part of Bigbasket's customer orders were picked here. The dry grocery items that were picked from METRO and Hypercity would be shipped to the Safal hub. At this hub, customer orders were segregated. During the early days, Abhinay and Ramesh were personally involved in the sorting and segregation.

Building Customer Centricity into Processes

Customer centricity was built into several processes. Most physical stores carried a line at the bottom of their invoices—'Goods once sold cannot be returned'. Bigbasket stood for a 'no questions asked' return policy from day one. If a customer bought a pack of five apples and had a complaint about the quality of one of the five apples a week after purchase, the price charged for the one apple would be refunded to the customer's e-wallet immediately. The customer service agent who took the call was empowered to do this. Bigbasket also offered a delivery guarantee, which meant that if an order delivery was delayed, Bigbasket would pay the customer 10 per cent of the order value. Rigorous review of how we were doing on each of these metrics gave us a good sense of the health of the business from the point of view of customer experience.

Some of the competitors had built a better user interface / user experience (UI/UX) when it came to the app features, but Bigbasket believed that this was not what customers were worried about the most. Fill rates and covering difficult categories were far more important. Some of the Board members who had invested in new-age e-commerce companies and knew the importance of UI/UX would bring up this issue from time to time. But, the Bigbasket founders were resolute in their belief that while this was important, it was not the most critical thing that needed fixing. The UI/UX received focused attention slightly later and was made seamless, but many of the start-ups that paid disproportionate attention to the UI/UX at the start of their journey did not eventually survive.

Dealing with Customer Fraud

The Analytics team at Bigbasket was accustomed to receiving requests for data from different functions. The functions needed to validate their hypotheses when they encountered a problem and needed the data for this purpose. Often, the way they framed their problem statement was incorrect or at times the team was even solving a wrong problem. The Analytics team saw its role as more than mere providers of data. After M.S. Subramanian came on board as the head of Analytics, he built on this belief and helped drive the culture of thoughtfully framing problem statements. When functions would come with requests for data, his question to them would be, 'What do you need this data for?', and through a series of questions, they would figure out whether this was the data they should be looking for at all in the first place. Often the one requesting for data would realise that they were asking a wrong question or framing the hypothesis incorrectly.

Of late, the Operations team had noticed an increasing trend of customers reporting missing items long after their orders were delivered. While there were a few genuine cases, the majority of the cases weren't. The current Bigbasket refund policy did not stipulate any expiry date for claiming refunds for missing items.

A quick analysis showed that nearly 10 per cent of such complaints came from customers who reported missing items 45 days after their order was delivered. This was hard to understand, especially since a majority of the complaints came from a small number of customers.

The Analytics team concluded correctly that a few customers were abusing the policy. So, their recommendation to the Operations team was to restrict the period customers could report missing items to a week.

The question Vipul Parekh and V.S. Sudhakar had asked was whether we should redesign the process to completely prevent abuse and possibly inconvenience a lot of genuine customers, or live with a certain percentage of abuse and make life easy and convenient for the majority of customers who were honest. When the Analytics team looked at data, they found that the percentage of customers who were misusing this was in the low single digits. When viewed with this lens, it didn't make sense to clamp down hard on this abuse.

This episode is a reflection of the larger customer-centric thinking in everything the company did—product quality, range, refund policies, guarantees, promotions and more. The customer was the centre of the Bigbasket universe.

Over the years this has led to a culture where any change that impacted a customer—in policy, levy of new fees, changes in product features, etc.— had to be preceded by a deep dive and pilots. Anyone doing anything that impacted the customers were urged to stand in the customer's shoes and see things from that perspective.

In Conclusion

Obsession with customer centricity at Bigbasket is deep. The same philosophy extended to internal customers. Even internal service providers were acutely aware that they were serving customers. There were only two types of teams at Bigbasket, namely those who served paying customers and those who served those who served paying customers. A product manager could not say no to a feature that business requested for without giving it a serious thought. The HR manager couldn't just turn down a request with a bureaucratic 'the policy doesn't allow this' kind of response. Better empathy was expected and every policy had to be reviewed periodically based on how effective it had been.

4
The Myths of E-Commerce Retail

You can only make sense of the online world by going offline and by getting the wisdom and emotional clarity to know how to make the best use of the Internet.

—Pico Iyer

Amazon accounts for nearly half of all e-commerce sales in the US. The remaining 50 per cent is accounted for by a long tail of large offline players like Apple, Walmart, Macy's, Home Depot, Best Buy, Costco and the like. This piece of data often comes as a surprise to many people—that 50 per cent of all e-commerce is controlled by predominantly offline companies.

E-commerce comes in many hues and shades. When you buy a movie ticket online, you are engaging in e-commerce. You are also engaging in e-commerce when you order grocery on the Bigbasket app or book a taxi on the Uber app. And, you are also engaging in it when you place an order online on Lenskart and visit an offline Lenskart store to pick up your product.

Let us start with the three most common myths about e-commerce.

Myth 1: E-commerce Means Discounts and Cashbacks

When Uber and Ola started operations, both customers and drivers had a whale of a time. India was new to online commerce of any kind. Most people didn't understand how these companies could offer such low fares and still make money. Very few understood that they did not want to make money in the short term. Their game plan was for the long term. It was about changing customer behaviour, getting them hooked to a great experience and gradually increasing the fares.

Right now, the good days are behind us. Consumer behaviour has undergone the change that these companies were hoping for. The taxi aggregation companies have now upped fares sharply, introduced charges for waiting time in traffic and created surge pricing during peak hours. The pricing is not transparent. Some customers have logged out and gone back to traditional means of public commute, but a good number of them have been hooked and continue to use their services despite the opacity in pricing.

So, cashbacks and discounts were a channel-switching strategy. It was backed by investors with deep pockets who were not willing to wait it out. They wanted to accelerate this switch and believed that any money spent in making this happen would only increase the overall returns.

Now let us move from taxi aggregation to retail e-commerce. Taxi aggregation was a green-field territory. There was no taxi service that existed prior to Uber or Ola in most Indian cities, including large metros like Bengaluru, Chennai, Hyderabad and Delhi. Kolkata and Mumbai had hail-a-taxi services, but the density of cabs on the road was so low that it was very difficult to get one. So taxi aggregators were not providing an alternative to an existing service. By eliminating the challenge of getting a cab reliably at a short notice at your doorstep, or wherever you wanted it, the new model was creating an on-demand taxi service. If taxi aggregators were a mere alternative to an existing service, consumers could go back to the other service if and when

Ola chose to raise prices. But, there was no alternative to go back to.

In retail, the reality was different. There was a very strong network of modern retail and 'kirana' stores, which were doing a good job of fulfilling the customer's needs. So, online retail would have to fight much harder. Attracting customers through discounts did not mean that customers would stick to online even after discounts were withdrawn; unlike in the case of Uber or Ola, they could easily go back to their earlier channels. The online value proposition was not strong enough without discounts. The trade-off was obvious—'convenience' of online versus the 'touch and feel' of offline. The balance was fine. It was discounts that were tilting the scales. The existing channels were no pushovers either. They would not capitulate without a fight. They would do everything within their power to thwart the online channel including mobilising political opinion against online businesses.

We believe there is an exception to this trade-off between 'convenience' and 'touch and feel'. Grocery is a category where 'touch and feel' is not critical. So, migration to online is bound to happen sooner or later. Within the grocery segment, we have noticed that fruits and vegetables have an element of 'touch and feel' and hence has been the hardest category. Bigbasket has cracked this too, through better sourcing, innovation in cold chains and faster transit from farm to the customer's home. We have discussed this in greater detail in the chapter—'From Farm to Fork to Nirvana'.

Myth 2: E-commerce Can Get You Super-Profits

The biggest problem with e-commerce has been that customers do not get a chance to touch and feel a product before purchase. A fraudulent customer could also claim that a wrong product was delivered and the supplier did not have a conclusive mechanism to settle this dispute. In a brick-and-mortar store when the customer walked out, it was implicit that she had seen and found the product satisfactory. The small print also said that 'goods once sold cannot be returned'. E-commerce businesses, therefore, saw very high returns. To promote and create trust in this new channel, online companies had to have a very liberal return policy, and every return added to costs in a significant way.

The cost of customer acquisition is high. Unless it could be amortised over multiple purchases, it was not sustainable. And if there is no differentiation, there is no loyalty or repeat purchases. Further, creating an optimal logistics network with reasonable operating costs is not easy and it doesn't come cheap.

Myth 3: It Is Easy to Scale an Online Business

Investors poured money into e-commerce with the belief that new and yet unestablished brands could extend their reach exponentially with an online presence. In addition, they assumed that all costs related to inventory and store rentals, often at premium spots in the city, would vanish. All you needed, they thought, were a few strategically located warehouses in the country with customer orders being dispatched through a hub-and-spoke model or national shipping. Offline stores also had a discoverability problem, which they believed an online presence would address.

Many of the assumptions proved to be wrong. As always, reality dawned after the hype had died down. When an offline entity chose to list on a marketplace, the challenges related to scaling or geographical reach of offline stores did not automatically go away. In some cases, nothing changed; in some cases there was improvement and for others, things deteriorated.

Theoretically, technology does help in increasing reach, but as long as the reach does not translate to visibility, discoverability and real transactions, it is of no use. For instance, the discoverability problem still remains when an offline entity makes a foray online via a marketplace. There were hundreds of sellers with similar or identical products and it was not easy for customers to discover you existed or what your reputation was. The problem of being lost in the crowd remained unresolved.

To enhance discoverability, those that came online had to start online advertising and pay the marketplace or Google for their name to bubble up on the top in a search. Search engine optimisation (SEO) and search engine marketing (SEM) became new sought-after skills. Even after all this, the discoverability may not improve significantly, and even if it does, customers may not trust you enough to transact online. A lot of the advertising metrics were fake. In October 2018, several advertisers filed a suit against Facebook for significant overstatements of the time users spent watching videos on their platform. It appeared only Google and Facebook were making money out of SEM with questionable outcomes for the advertisers trying to enhance visibility and discoverability.

The Real Question Is, 'Where Does E-commerce Go from Here?'

E-commerce comes in many forms and shapes:

- First of all, you can have an online marketplace where its role is to bring buyers and sellers on a common technology platform and provide some essential services like logistics, advertising and payment solutions. There can be a charge for users of such services. Alibaba took this position. The role of a technology-driven platform is to increase discoverability and enhance the ease of doing business. The sellers who list on such a marketplace may or may not have an offline presence.

- An offline business need not list on a marketplace if they have a strong reach and a loyal customer base. They can create their own exclusive online business. Walmart and Apple are examples.
- You could have a company that has only an online presence and still does not list on a marketplace. Bigbasket is an example. Such a company may choose to not have an offline presence or may figure out at some point that an extension to offline would serve customers better.
- Offline to online and vice versa will be the norm. Take the case of Amazon's foray into grocery. In the US, it acquired a large offline chain called Whole Foods. Lenskart and Zivame started online and extended to offline, while an offline retail chain like Walmart extended its presence the other way round.

The inevitable conclusion is that online or e-commerce is just another channel.

The retail business has grappled with channels and their conflicts since its existence. When modern retail—large-format stores—began emerging in India, there were fears that the kirana stores would die. That did not happen. Both thrived and both grew. The share of modern retail after more than two decades is an abysmal 10 per cent.

Technology has given shape to a new channel. The struggle between the channels will continue with one new channel in the mix. The power swings will happen from time to time.

But just as modern retail did not live up to predictions of total domination, online retail too, will not live up to such a prophecy. Companies, both online and offline, have now wisely begun to take a holistic view of channels from a customer's perspective.

The Emergence of Store Brands

Would you replace your favorite brand of soap or shampoo you use every day with unbranded products? Off the bat, most people will respond with a resounding 'no'. Instead of shampoo and soap, if the products were toothpaste and a packet of sugar what would be your response? In all likelihood, you would be open to unbranded sugar and may not yet be okay with unbranded toothpaste.

So, it is obvious that some products are more amenable to being commoditised, and hence unbranded, compared to other products. A product like flour that most of us would believe could easily be commoditised has defied this belief. Aashirwaad is a brand of flour that has totally wiped out all other brands. No private label has dared to take on Aashirwaad. This brand by ITC has become pretty iconic because the brand's team is obsessed with the quality of flour that would deliver the perfect end product—rotis that would remain soft several hours after baking.

The tussle between the power of brands and the power of distribution has been an old one. Over the decades, as retail got corporatised and large chains began emerging, store brands began making a presence. With mounting real estate costs, retail chains had to think of innovative ways of improving margins. So far, they were stocking big brands on their shelves. Consumer companies that controlled these brands created a pull for their brands through a combination of product quality, promotion, price and place (the classic 4 Ps).

At some point, the retail chains began wondering whether they should create their own brands. These brands were unlikely to be as powerful as the regular brands and were not expected to create a strong customer pull, but this could be more than compensated by giving them much more visibility in the stores. The regular brands were about creating 'pull' and store brands could be about creating 'push'. These store brands could be priced much lower because there would be no advertising and other associated brand-building costs. Store brands started by establishing their presence in categories where differentiation was difficult like staples and other food products. Gradually, the retail chains figured out that they could create store brands in most categories, though some would be more difficult than the others.

As someone once observed, 'After mastering the art of selling everyone else's stuff, retail chains and marketplaces began persuading shoppers to buy their own stuff.'

If physical retail chains could create store brands by leveraging their access to customers and through reach, why wouldn't marketplaces at some point think of creating their own online store brands. This has begun happening. Apparel is a category where fit and style are of paramount importance and hence the entry barriers are limited especially if good designs can be distributed at low costs. Amazon has close to 80 private labels and has raced ahead of Macy's in apparel, a category in which the latter had been the undisputed leader. As a competitive strategy, Macy's has been trying to offer more brands that consumers can't get anywhere else. It has tried to adapt quickly by evolving into an omni-channel retailer.

It is not without reason that brands have existed for as long as they have. Brands deliver clear and sharp value propositions for their target consumer segments. Consumers associate a certain imagery, and often derive an identity, from the brands they are associated with. This fulfills an inherent human need and hence brands are unlikely to be displaced easily. Having said this, brands that do not have a strong value proposition are more likely to be displaced by private brands of retail chains and distribution companies. The battle between 'Brands' and 'Brandless' will be epic.

Regulators Step in

When a new channel shows patience and allows consumers to switch voluntarily at their natural pace without any inducements, the switch can happen without much acrimony and a new order can take shape seamlessly. However, this is often a long-drawn-out process and consumers could take their own time, depending on how strong the value proposition of the new channel is vis-à-vis the older channels. If a channel is perceived to be using access to deep pockets to force a switch quickly, and in the process, disrupting an existing ecosystem, the change won't happen without a fight.

You can see this happening in India, and the rest of the world as well.

Arguments against inducements for switching channels can be easily challenged because it is against free-market principles. Arguments for allowing market forces a free run can also be challenged because it can kill smaller players without access to capital and talent.

Capitalism, as well as the society, had evolved fairly quickly to achieve this fine balance by instituting mechanisms that created a level playing field. Every country has legislation on regulating monopolistic tendencies.

So, the regulators in India have a tough job. The balance they had to make was protecting existing players from going out of business overnight and in the process cause bloodshed and disruption versus promoting innovation. Some light regulation is absolutely necessary, but over-regulating a nascent sector can kill innovation. We hope that the regulators can maintain this fine balance.

In Conclusion

Retail has been evolving, but technology, and Amazon in particular, has accelerated the pace of innovation. The evolution has branched off in multiple directions. A marketplace like Amazon has acquired a large offline chain to make a foray into grocery. Marketplaces are creating their own strong brands and private labels. Predominantly offline businesses are making a foray into the online platform and vice versa. Some have chosen pure-play online and some others have chosen pure-play offline.

Online is just another channel in the whole scheme of things. Every retail company is trying to find its feet to incorporate this new channel into their overall channel strategy.

5

Haute Couture Is Passé

Fashion is like eating, you shouldn't stick to the same menu.

—Kenzo Takada

Over the last decade or so, food had slowly replaced haute couture to become the new fashion. Food habits and tastes have begun to make greater social statements than apparel and luxury goods. India has clearly been on the move. This had implications on how Bigbasket built its business. The assortment selection, supply chain, warehouses, cold chains, farmer-connect programmes and international sourcing all had to be designed keeping in mind rapidly changing consumer preferences.

The Green Revolution in the 1950s was motivated by the immediate food security needs of a newly independent India. It focused on basic cereals like wheat and rice (carbohydrates), which constituted around 40 per cent of the food energy requirements of an average Indian (2,800 kcal per day).

The mix of what Indians eat has changed in the last 50 years. A few key call-outs in the change are:

- Indians consume 22 per cent more calories now per day vis-à-vis 50 years ago.
- The share of protein (including protein from meats) has grown.
- The share of cereals has decreased.
- The fall in the share of grains has happened alongside increase in sugar and fat intake.

As Indian society became more affluent, we saw a shift to dairy- and animal-based proteins. As people are becoming more health-conscious, they are shifting to diets that are low in carbohydrates, but high in protein, vitamins and minerals. This health consciousness is also a by-product of affluence.

Shame in Millets No More

Growing up, Mahesh Rao lived in Bengaluru's upmarket suburb of Sadashivnagar. In the years of his childhood, millets were considered a taboo on the dining table. Millets formed the staple diet of farmers and low-income families in Karnataka. You couldn't afford to have your friends see you having traditional millet dishes.

Mahesh soon became a very successful engineer who worked for more than two decades at Boeing's factory in Seattle as an aeronautical engineer. But, he had returned to settle down in his hometown. Every day at dinner, he was served millet pudding. There was no shame in consuming millets any more. His success on the world stage had given him enough confidence to erase his childhood complex about millets. Millets are now considered a superfood; they are also gluten-free. At the same time, these crops are mainly rain-fed, with very little water or other requirements. Thus, these grains are both healthy as well as good for the environment. Millets were, until recently, considered a poor man's food or bird feed and could never be seen in the kitchens or dining tables of the affluent in India. However, now they are considered cool and trendy. We have come a full circle 60 years after the Green Revolution.

Fruits and Vegetables Overtake Cereals

Another clear shift we have seen is in the consumption of fruits and vegetables. India's horticulture production surpassed cereal production for the first time in 2014. The trend continues unabated. Fruit consumption is growing both in terms of the quantity as well as varieties. Hitherto unknown fruits like kiwi, dragon fruit, rambutan and avocado as well as vegetables like lettuce, pak choi, coloured capsicum, kale, rocket leaves and zucchini are being consumed in increasing quantities. Also, rare apple varieties like Fuji, Gala and Granny have become commonplace now. The quality is improving on the strength of better pre- and post-harvest practices. Horticulture crops generally give a better return to the farmer when compared to field crops. One of the reasons for growth in consumption of fruits and vegetables is the epidemiological evidence, which shows an association between the consumption of more than 400 grams of fruit and vegetables per day and a reduced risk of certain diet-related chronic diseases, such as cardiovascular diseases, stroke and some cancers.

Imports have played a major role in reshaping consumer expectations around quality, seasonality and price of certain fruits. Apples are a case in point. Today, India imports over 3 lakh metric tonnes of apples, besides the domestic production of around 20 lakh metric tonnes. These imports motivate the domestic industry to improve quality, variety, productivity and remain competitive. The import duty of around 50 per cent ensures that there is a level playing field for our farmers. It also brings in over $500 million in additional revenue to the exchequer.

The shift from core cereals and pulses to fruits, vegetables, poultry, dairy, piggery, fishery and beekeeping reflects changing consumer trends.

Explosion of Choice

If you just rewind back to about 15 years, the best store would have an assortment of 3,000 stock keeping units (SKUs) and customers would line up in queues to shop there. That number has now jumped up nearly seven times to over 20,000 SKUs. A simple malt drink that was used to supplement the diet of children was priced at ₹200 per kilogram (at today's equivalent price) and that was sufficient 15 years ago. Now, some malt drinks with protein supplements come at ₹1,000 per kilogram and many parents are happy to buy this for their children.

Juices were very rudimentary and moderately priced. The choices have continuously expanded. Today, cold-pressed juices are the rage because studies conclusively show that when the normal process for extracting juice is deployed, some nutrients are destroyed because of the heat. Cold chains have been created to move cold-pressed juices from the place of manufacture to different parts of the country.

The advent of modern trade in India around 20 years ago allowed the creation of strong and deep supply chains that led to national distribution. The shift from regional to national distribution allowed consumers in every part of the country to experience food (and other) products from across the country. The advent of e-commerce took this a notch higher by strengthening national distribution significantly and accessing international supply chains.

The big shift in cereals has been an explosion in the number of brands. Except for a few brands, most food was unbranded earlier and sold as commodities. Rice was rice, wheat was wheat and tea was tea. Branding allowed differentiation in terms of ingredients and other value-adds as well as packaging. This allowed premium pricing. Brands now cater to micro markets and tastes, and are highly personalised.

Gourmet and Organic Come of Age

Another area where there has been a sea change in consumer habits is gourmet foods. Chocolates, until 20 years ago, meant just those indigenously made by Cadbury's; same applied to ice cream. Today, the range of chocolates and ice creams available is mind-boggling. At Bigbasket, the sale of gourmet products went up a hundredfold in just three years. The variety of cheeses, sourced internationally, that are available and consumed would shock anyone from the previous generation. Vinegar consumption has gone up almost 500-fold in the last three years and so has the consumption of olive oil. People of Indian origin returning from foreign shores to participate in India's economic growth have brought in the food habits cultivated there and have played a significant role in influencing tastes and habits.

There is a growing consumer segment that has a strong preference for organically-grown food. The market for milk produced from cows that have been fed an organic diet without any hormonal injections is growing. Whole farms devoted to producing organic food are sprouting across the country.

Indians Take to International Cuisines

The changing habits also reflect in the explosion of exotic and niche restaurants serving every kind of global cuisine, especially in tier 1 cities. Italian restaurants were most popular to begin with because there were some underlying similarities with Indian cuisine in terms of usage of herbs, fresh vegetables and dairy. Mexican food was the next rage because of the spicy nature of the cuisine, which resonated with the Indian palate. Chinese restaurants had been around the longest, but the food they dished out was hardly

Chinese. It was highly customised for Indian tastes so much so that no Chinese would acknowledge it as Chinese food. However, now there has been a spurt in Chinese restaurants serving genuine cuisine. You can easily find restaurants that specialise in Indonesian, Vietnamese, Caribbean, Korean, French and Spanish cuisines. If one looks around a little, it's not hard to find restaurants exclusively serving sushi or Kobe beef. This growing diversity in the restaurant network is supported by a large supply chain that sources the raw materials and ingredients in containers from different parts of the world.

Masterchef Australia has the greatest viewership in India followed by *Masterchef Canada,* among cooking shows. *Masterchef India* is a distant third. More and more youth are now taking up culinary courses, specialising in international cuisines; becoming a chef is now a cool thing.

Another food trend that has emerged in the last few years is the coming together of food and technology. This emerging area of e-commerce enables instant gratification for those willing to pay for food at any time of the day without having to exert any effort.

In Conclusion

Food is the first thing people splurge on, when income levels rise, followed by apparel, housing and education. Indian food habits are going global and one of the unintended outcomes is that Indians, especially the affluent ones, are becoming susceptible to all types of food allergies that the western world is going through.

Food is also becoming the most abused addiction. In our opinion, India is soon going to be the snacks capital of the world. Chocolate and ice cream have become standard stress busters. Children have begun to have a bigger role in influencing food habits because of the greater impact of

TV advertising, and companies have begun to tailor-make food products for children. Increasing consumption of processed, branded and imported food products has been a strong trend.

A deeper understanding of all these trends went into the way different pieces of the Bigbasket business were conceived and built.

6
From Farm to Fork to Nirvana

We have traversed a path few have dared to. We are continuing on a path still fewer have the courage to follow. We must pursue a path that even fewer can dream to pursue [...] because we hold in trust the aims and aspirations of millions of our countrymen.

—Dr Verghese Kurien

Author Simon Sinek popularised a well-known and an extremely powerful thought process by giving it a concise title—'Start with Why'.

We have almost always started with the 'why' before getting down to the 'what' and the 'how', but nowhere is this approach as pronounced and apparent as it is in our fruits and vegetables (F&V) journey.

Why Do We Do F&V at All When No One Else Is Doing It?

Bigbasket chose to have F&V in the assortment because if customers could only buy dry grocery online and had to visit a physical store for their F&V requirement, the entire proposition of 'convenience' would be in ruins. The principal value proposition of online grocery was to avoid a visit to the store.

When the 'why' is so compelling and strong, then however difficult the 'what' and 'how' might be, they need to be figured out.

The quality of a packet of Surf Excel is exactly the same whether you buy it from a kirana store in a small provincial town or from a hip department store in Bengaluru. The supply chain for most branded products, with reasonably long shelf lives, is relatively simple, evolved and mature. The problem is creating a supply chain to handle perishable products like F&V.

Bigbasket realised early on that if they could crack the F&V problem, they would have built an unassailable moat.

Touch and Feel

Just picture this in your mind—you walk into the F&V section of a retail store to buy spinach. Bundles of spinach are neatly arranged on the shelf. You don't just pick up a few bundles randomly. You instinctively look for freshness and quality of the leaf before picking the bundles you want to buy. Take a completely different case now. Let's assume that you were expecting some guests the next day and wanted five kilograms of Alphonso mangoes. You would pick all the ripe and juicy fruit. Instead, if you had no guests and you planned to consume the fruit over the next seven days, you might pick a couple of ripe and juicy ones and the rest a little raw so that they would ripen over the week. If you bought all ripe and juicy pieces, some of them would not last the week. So, the choice is based on the context that is very personal to the customer. If a customer ordered five kilograms of Alphonso mangoes online, how would the online company know whether to pick all ripe fruit or some ripe and some that would ripen over the week? Or imagine buying okra or ladies' fingers. You are likely to touch and feel each piece to check for tenderness before adding it to the basket.

In F&V purchases, the customer always did the picking and the final quality check at the store. If a customer had to order F&V online, she had to be sure that the company would do exactly the same quality checks as rigorously as she would have done them if she had visited the store herself.

One of the questions that the F&V team at Bigbasket continues to ask themselves daily is, 'What more can we do to eliminate the need for this touch and feel and win the trust of our online customers?'

Cut Fruits and Vegetables

Let's stand in the customer's shoes once again for a moment. What does she do with the fruits and vegetables she buys? She chops them for consumption or use them for preparing dishes like sambaar. Would she like it if we could supply chopped F&V? Would she like it even better if we supplied her all the chopped vegetables in the right proportion that she could use directly for the sambaar?

The answers are clearly 'yes'. But, there are questions she would have. Would the chopping be done under hygienic conditions? Would any artificial preservatives be used to maintain freshness? Would these preservatives be harmful or would they spoil the flavour? Would the prices be reasonable?

We addressed all these questions. We kept the pricing very reasonable and just about covered the natural wastage during chopping. We tied up with the Central Food Technology and Research Institute (CFTRI) at Mysuru and signed licence agreements with them for usage of relevant technology. Bigbasket has over 100 SKUs for just cut vegetables now. This has added to customer convenience significantly. We rapidly expanded into ready-to-eat assortment of fruits, both in family and single-serve packs, thus promoting healthy snacking.

The 'why' was always the starting point.

The Man Behind This All

Vipul Mittal graduated from the Institute of Rural Management, Anand in 1991 and his first job was with the Anand Milk Union Limited, more popularly known as Amul, in Gujarat. The year 1991 was also when India embarked on the path of economic reforms. The dairy cooperatives were in a bit of a quandary, given the possibility of deep pocketed competition from well-entrenched MNCs, which probably also had better technologies and product range. In 1992, Amul appointed B.M. Vyas as the managing director. His youthful energy, vision and dynamism became the stuff of legends.

The next decade or so was a period of great transformation for Amul as it braced itself for competition from the likes of Nestlé and Unilever. This period gave Vipul unique perspectives on strategy, change management as well as marketing. At Amul, customer centricity in decision-making was religion. Amul ensured that a fair price to farmers for their produce along with a reasonable sale price for the end consumer was maintained while still running a profitable business. This was made possible by keeping a close check on the costs. Focus on cost and execution was unparalleled and was, to some extent, achieved by centralisation of decision-making.

At Amul, Vyas would encourage everyone to think out of the box, on a global scale and challenge existing paradigms. Vipul learnt and honed some of these skills at Amul and applied them to great effect at Bigbasket.

One of the reasons for Vipul coming on board was that he saw a very similar set of beliefs at Bigbasket. The founders were leaders with vision, passion, commitment and patience. Customer understanding and centricity was exactly like what he had seen at Amul.

Before Vipul's induction into Bigbasket, F&V was being run by D.V. Giri. Giri had worked for over five years at METRO Cash & Carry in the Buying and Merchandising (B&M) team. He had also been the business head for Private Labels at Nilgiris Retail and was recruited to head Merchandising at Bigbasket in March 2012. Giri helped in laying the foundation for the F&V category. Vipul was recruited to head the F&V category in December 2014. Together, they were a formidable combination.

Learning from Amul

One of the challenges in F&V was to shorten the transit time from the farm to the customer's home. We realised it was wise to do business with the farmers directly and ship the produce from the farm to our distribution centres both from a perishability as well as margin-improvement perspective. These are called dark stores because customers do not walk into them. When we gave this a deeper thought, we figured out that the programme would fail unless we also considered enhancing the livelihoods of the farmers as a key objective.

Farmer-connect Programmes

Our perspectives changed when enhancing farmer livelihoods became one of the core objectives of our farmer-connect programme. Based on this objective, we laid out some very fundamental rules of engagement. Mutual trust and financial well-being would be the bedrock of our farmer relationships. Let us illustrate this point with an example. When there is a glut in the market, the prices of perishables could plummet to a level that is much lower than the cost price. However, our procurement price, irrespective of how low the prevailing market price may be, is never lower than the one-and-a-half times the cost price of the farmer. In other words, the farmer is assured of a profit margin of at least 50 per cent. This is pretty much the formula that the government uses to determine the minimum support price (MSP) for various commodities.

We started off by setting up collection centres (CCs) in the rural areas to source vegetables from the farms. They are sorted, graded, weighed and accounted for in the farmer's presence at the CC and the payment is sent directly to the farmer's bank account within 48 hours. We also deploy agronomists to monitor the progress of the crops from 'seed to harvest' as per a pre-decided package of practices. From a customer perspective, we are an online commerce company. We subsequently extended the digital connect at the back end to our farmers. We use a third-party software called Smartfarm to manage the farmer database and monitor the growing activity from seed to harvest. This allows us to standardise the package of practices for various crops and ensure safe food for our customer with residue levels of chemicals within the prescribed limits.

We also use an in-house app to capture market prices and share the data with our CCs. The farmer payment process, facilitated by technology, helps us maintain transparency and deal with a large number of them. They are very comfortable dealing with us on a one-to-one basis because of the trust we have built.

Going forward, we will be using an app to communicate the demand for the next day and allow farmers to reserve their produce against this demand. This would increase the predictability of business for the farmers and help them plan better.

We digitised the process of farmer monitoring as well as price discovery to bring in complete transparency for all stakeholders and remove discretion from critical decision-making. Today, we are proud that over 70 per cent of our fresh produce is purchased outside the Agricultural Produce Market Committee (APMC) markets (or mandis as they are more popularly known) and directly from the farmers.

Cooperative Within a Corporate

Today, we have more than 35 CCs across the country. Amul was a farmer cooperative where they were not just stakeholders but owners as well. We used some of the principles of a cooperative in running our farmer-connect programmes. We virtually run a cooperative within a corporate.

We have created extensive storage and transport infrastructure to ship the produce in the freshest and fastest possible manner to our distribution centres and dark stores, and onward to the customer. The prices of agricultural commodities are discovered across mandis in the country. They largely depend on the dynamics of demand-supply in respective markets for the day. This opens an opportunity for geographical arbitrage. With our national presence, distribution centres across 25 cities and CCs across 35 locations, we have created a complex national grid to ship produce from one market to the other, and balance the prices. Simultaneously, we also store commodities like onions, potatoes and apples to ensure availability in the off season for our customers.

Contract farming has mostly been used by the processing industry in India. As a model, it has the potential to remove some of the risk factors associated with farming. The flip side is upholding the contracts with the farmers in case of upward price movement in the market. We have initiated contract farming for exotic vegetables and also make many erstwhile seasonal vegetables available throughout the year.

Innovative pricing models are being explored to expand this model.

Fruits, in general, have a better shelf life and better value realisation when compared to vegetables. We focused on climacteric fruits and ensured carbide-free, safe ripening for our customers. The climacteric is a stage of fruit ripening associated with increased ethylene production and a rise in cellular respiration. Apples, bananas, melons, apricots and tomatoes are climacteric fruits. Citrus, grapes and strawberries are not.

We introduced mechanised grading and BRIX—sugar acid ratio testing—for most of our fruits to ensure a consistent size and taste experience. We set up an integrated packing house at Ananthapur, in the state of Andhra Pradesh, in September 2017 to aggregate the fruits and ship them across the country. We also initiated direct imports in December 2017 to increase our exposure and control the availability, cost and quality of key imported fruits as well as to introduce new global range across the seasons. Our fixation with disintermediation will continue with Bigbasket working closely with farmers and farmer groups across the globe.

Defining Strategy

In one of the meetings, Sudhakar asked Vipul Mittal, 'Why can't we sell all the organic F&Vs at the same price as the conventional F&Vs?' At the same meeting, there was another question, 'Why can't we have the same F&V quality as TESCO in the UK?' One of the Nobel laureates in an acceptance speech had said that his mother never asked him what he learnt at school. She always asked him what good question he had asked that day. Insightful questions have a way of clearing cobwebs and nudging us in the right direction.

Both these questions got Vipul thinking. In one of my several conversations with him, this is what he had to say, 'Let me admit that no one has ever brought such a disruptive thought process to this domain until now. So much about F&V is taken for granted in most retail companies that any semblance of scientific enquiry and challenge is often greeted with defensiveness. Thanks to all my past leaders, wonderful learning at Amul and the maturity of the years [he was 45 at the time], I dealt with these questions with the respect they deserved. The quest for finding better answers to many of these questions continues to guide most of our innovations till date.'

Organic F&V: Genuine or a Marketing Ploy?

Our quest for an answer soon led us to a disturbing fact. Savvy marketers had hit upon 'organic' as a marketing tool to make more margins, rather than use it to create sustainable and natural living. The belief that organic products would naturally be premium-priced was so deep even among the consumers that all efforts to bridge the price differential were met with huge resistance. In an attempt to demolish the paradigm of price premium for organic F&V, we started scouting the landscape for organic sources. In the process, we hit a steep learning curve. We quickly realised that if we had to make organic the norm, it was important to reach out to the farmers directly. Especially farmers in the remotest areas, where organic may still be the norm rather than the exception. We recruited two fresh graduates from the GKVK College of Agricultural Science in Bengaluru in 2015, who had interacted with organic farmer groups during their coursework, and gave them the task of starting organic collection centres in their respective areas. Mohan Kumar started the one in Mysuru and Sandeep Munjhane in north Karnataka.

In our journey to strengthen our organic offerings, we met some truly amazing and passionate individuals who helped sharpen our understanding of the topic. One such person was Patanjali Jha, a senior bureaucrat who motivated us to introduce fresh raw turmeric (amrutaballi or neem giloy) and aloe vera in our assortment. His conviction in the therapeutic value of these items was so infectious that we were probably the first, and only, retailer to introduce these products and continue to sell them till date.

Recently, we gave a big push to tender coconut, thus offering a natural beverage in natural packaging to our customers in an easy-to-open format and making it very affordable. We sell more than 20,000 tender coconut pieces every day.

Start-up Within a Start-up: Our Unique Structure

Bigbasket has a strong B&M function. B&M is an integral part of any retail company. It is further structured by category; they could be FMCG, Staples, Gourmet, etc. Each one is led by a category head. Since F&V is a category, we had the choice of plugging it in B&M. However, we chose to run it separately as a start-up within a start-up. The head of B&M, Seshu Kumar, was the one who actually came up with this idea since it was difficult to bake this business into the standard mold of a retail B&M function. We do not have established vendors in F&V with whom we can sign Terms of Trade (TOTs) that include pricing, quality, fill rates, etc. Conventional vendors work with retail companies (in this case, Bigbasket) and periodically do promotional campaigns to drive sales and growth. In the absence of such vendors in F&V, the only way of giving a consistent experience to our customers and build a sustainable business was to do all of this in-house. And that is what we did.

Innovation Is the Key

One of the first tasks that was assigned early on to the F&V team in 2015 was to minimise the use of plastic and reduce the cost of packaging, both at the same time. The F&V team assigned this task to a bright intern, Ayan Deb, from a leading business school. Very soon, Bigbasket moved most of the packaging to paper and biodegradable corn starch bags. This reduced the use of plastics by over 48 per cent and the cost by over 16 per cent. As the nature of our business (home delivery) demands that all items are packed for the consumer, we keep exploring more and more eco-friendly and cost-effective alternatives. Our initial decision to use customer-friendly returnable crates has played a big role in minimising the use of unnecessary packaging material.

In 2016, an Innovations team, under Praful Thachery, was formed at Bigbasket. Praful was a co-founder of Delyver, a company that Bigbasket had acquired in late 2015. The scope of the Innovations team was broad—it ranged from automating warehouse operations to improving the quality of F&V using technology. One of the first tasks entrusted to this team was to help ensure consistent F&V quality for the customers irrespective of season. The quality in summer had to be the same as that in winter. After extensive research and trials, the team came up with a cost-effective cold chain solution.

The question was who could qualify to be on the Innovations team. The one-line job description that Hari Menon had for the recruiter was: 'We need someone like Tony Stark. We want people who love breaking down things and building them back again; someone who loves playing around with technology and solving problems.' We moved one of the most unconventional thinkers, Adarsha, from the Projects team to the Innovations team. We hired Navin who had a couple of years of experience, and Suraj, who had just passed out from an engineering college.

The Innovations team was also mandated with automating some of our sorting, grading and packing functions. The team also took upon themselves the task of rebooting F&V by introducing a tech-integration project called F&V 2.0. The objective of this project was to solve the multiple challenges of traceability and 'first-in, first-out' (FIFO) across the supply chain using robust technology.

This is a work in progress with some exciting results just around the corner.

The Road Ahead

Technology is rapidly changing the way we have been used to doing things. Agro-tech companies are beginning to provide reliable solutions for hitherto seemingly unsolvable issues. For example, there are companies that are using image processing technology to grade a given batch of potatoes so as to help discover their quality as well as a fair price for the buyer and the seller. We see ourselves engaged with most of these cutting-edge technologies to help enhance the customer experience as well as increase farmer income through transparency of engagements. We are incubating some of these initiatives being piloted by some start-ups as part of the Yes Bank's 'Yes Scale' programme.

In Conclusion

The future will see Bigbasket further deepening its engagement with the farmers. Farmers are a key stakeholder in our scheme of things. We are developing models to be able to pick the entire produce of the farmers and also do contract farming on a large scale. This would be facilitated by the new B2B verticals within Bigbasket, namely HORECA and Kirana; more on them later. It allows us to increase our volumes multifold and at the same time sell all the grades of F&V.

The other new businesses of BB Instant and BB Daily will also give a big boost to the F&V business, both in terms of customer convenience and increased volumes for the farmers. It would allow us to introduce a wider range of ready-to-eat and ready-to-cook F&V. Cold-pressed juices and tender coconut will compete with milk on the breakfast table.

India is the second largest producer of F&V at over 300 million tonnes per annum. Despite this, our per capita consumption of F&V at about 300 grams per person a day is still lower than the WHO-recommended 400 grams per person a day.

We want this to go up. We believe we can play our bit in making this happen. We are increasingly focusing on this bigger goal. We see F&V as the source of good physical health for our consumers and good commercial health for our farmers. It is our aspiration to be at the forefront of driving this revolution in the country.

At the end of the day, answering the 'why' thoughtfully was what helped Bigbasket build the F&V vertical in a way that no other company has been able to do.

7
Tech-Enabled, Not Tech-First

Technology, like art, is a soaring exercise of the human imagination.

—Daniel Bell

Most start-ups fall into one of two categories: a) those that are tech-first, where one of the co-founders is also the CTO. The perspective in these start-ups is often, 'How can we leverage technology to build new businesses?'; and b) those that are tech-enabled, where the CTO is almost always not a founder. The perspective here is, 'How can technology enhance the effectiveness of our business?'

By this yardstick, Bigbasket is a tech-enabled company. This is an outcome of design, accident and choice. Usually, accident and design, by definition, don't go together. While four of the five founders of Bigbasket are engineers by education, they had not worked in what today are commonly referred to as tech companies.

The founders were clear that Bigbasket was going to be an online retail company and not a tech company that also did retail. Given this context, the founders decided to learn tech and in March 2012 hired Pramod Jajoo as the CTO. This is something we have talked about in the first chapter in some detail.

Building for Scale: Phase 1

It was 12 September 2014. The email from Pramod to the Tech team said it all. Helion and Zodius Capital had decided to invest over ₹200 crore in Bigbasket. The Engineering team had 13 members and the overall company headcount was 50. Within a few days of the funding announcement, word began going around that a separate Product team was being constituted.

In less than a week, an internal communications mail went out, announcing the creation of a Product function. Three product teams were constituted:

- Website
- Front-end App
- Back end

Tanu Gupta, who had earlier worked with Infosys, Citibank and Commonfloor would lead the Website Product team, Hari Palapetti would lead the Front-end App, and Tejas Vyas, the Back end.

Bigbasket was not an app for groceries. It was a grocery company that had an app. And that is a big difference. What this meant was that there was a huge back end of warehouses, transshipment hubs, dark stores, etc., which went into fulfilling customers' orders. It was not just a marketplace. So, the Product for managing the back end was extremely critical and drove a big part of the customer experience and growth. Every time the operating model was tweaked, and it happened continually, the back-end changes on the Product side had to be made to enable these changes in the operating model. The back-end Product at Bigbasket continued to be the lifeline of the company in many ways.

The Bigbasket business model was a big hit with customers. The 100 per cent fill rate, the capability to deliver fruits and vegetables as well as chilled and frozen products was unheard of. Bigbasket had begun seeing exponential growth. Growth and constant tweaks to the business model needed to be propelled by some heavy engineering horsepower. The frugal structure, in which Pramod managed a bunch of tech leads and product managers, worked well for a while, but it soon started showing signs of cracking.

Pramod was virtually the sole engineering manager. A large part of his time at work went into dealing with operational and tactical issues, leaving very little room for strategic work. There were continuous delays in the roll-out of new features, along with an increase in breakdowns and stakeholder dissatisfaction.

Decision to Hire VPs for Engineering and Product

We took two decisions to fix this. We took a call to hire a vice president (VP) for Engineering to extract Pramod out of the day-to-day execution and firefighting. We also took the call to create separate Engineering teams for different modules and have each module or piece of work headed by an engineering manager.

Some of the Board members believed that the Bigbasket website and app were not as good as they should be. They believed that the apps of some of our competitors had a better UI/UX, and from time to time they would push for creation of a separate, and independent, role of head of Product. This had become the norm in almost all consumer Internet companies. The founders didn't fully agree that a role like this was needed.

Some of the structure options were: a) separate the Product and Tech functions completely and have a CTO and a chief product officer (CPO) independently report to Sudhakar, b) hire a VP, Product, who, along with the VP for Engineering, would report to Pramod, c) Hire a VP for Engineering and make no changes on the Product side where a bunch of product managers would continue to report to Pramod. In this structure, Pramod would have to continue to act as the de facto product head.

We finally picked the second option and we decided to hire a VP for Engineering and a VP for Product.

Raghu Chakravarthi and Chintan Mehta, both Yahoo veterans, were hired as the VPs for Engineering and Product respectively.

After making some progress and establishing the proof of concept for this structure, both Raghu and Chintan departed for personal reasons. We had to hire replacements.

Building for Scale: Phase 2

After a great deal of thought, we decided to elevate Tejas Vyas, who was the product manager responsible for the back end as the product head. We also took the call to hire a VP for Engineering from outside the company.

From a Thriving Career in a Global Powerhouse to Bigbasket

Rakshit Daga joined Bigbasket as VP and head of Engineering. He came with a rich experience leading large global Engineering teams. His technology career began in the US after he graduated from a master's programme. He worked for a few start-ups and eventually joined SAP in 2005. A sterling eight-year career with SAP in the US provided Rakshit with a variety of opportunities to develop competencies to build world-class Engineering/Product teams. Rakshit's career in SAP began with a role in the CEO's office as an architect. SAP is a large global organisation that builds enterprise software for large (and now small as well) businesses. While it is headquartered in Germany, it had a strong presence in the US. Rakshit's first job at SAP was linked to one of its legendary founders Hasso Plattner's then evolving belief in building products that incorporated design thinking. Access to the CEO's office came with its perks but also had its downsides—battles for acceptance of initiatives emerging from the CEO's office from business heads, and turf wars between departments because of overlap in work areas.

While Rakshit learnt considerably from the nearly three-year stint in the strategic role, he was looking to switch gears from executing strategic projects for the CEO to delivering products leveraging his engineering expertise. At an opportune moment, his former boss at his earlier start-up who had also joined SAP pulled Rakshit into the now well-known SAP Labs organisation. SAP Labs was designed to be SAP's R&D facility with operations across the globe. A few months into his new role, Rakshit was tasked with setting up a sub-team within SAP Labs called AppHaus (house of apps) that would build apps on top of the SAP platform. AppHaus was set up to work like a start-up even though it was part of a global organisation. A few months into this role, Rakshit's boss wanted to know if he would be interested in moving to Bengaluru to set up an AppHaus team in India. After some thought, Rakshit took on the challenge of moving himself and his family overseas. It seemed to be an opportune time to move to India both professionally and personally. Professionally, this was a great opportunity to manage a global team across India, China, US and Europe. Personally, it provided his kids the opportunity to study in India during their formative years while allowing Rakshit to be close to ageing parents.

The India that Rakshit came back to after a decade in the US was different from the country that he had left. He observed that the India he was returning to was a resurgent economy characterised by a young population. Rakshit tried replicating the start-up culture of AppHaus of the US in India as well and succeeded to a great extent. The one-year experiment of moving to India soon turned to a two-year stay. During that time, the entrepreneurial bug bit Rakshit. In partnership with a friend from his graduate school days in the US, Rakshit started a B2B start-up in Bengaluru. It ran well for some time but the challenges of managing cash flows caught up in 2017 and the team had to wind down operations. While it was not a success, it gave Rakshit a wealth of experience in running a start-up in a frugal manner, and working with a young but yet-to-mature software developer population in India.

The Man Behind the Bigbasket Product Journey

The one person who has had the biggest role in shaping the Bigbasket product journey is Tejas Vyas. If you wish to understand a product, you need to know the upbringing, values, beliefs and the life experiences of the designer.

Failure and Frustration

The emerald oligotrophic lake stood calm in the midst of breathtaking vistas. Glacial ice spilled into the lake and the entire Everest range peered at Tejas atop the Kongma La Pass at an altitude of 5,400 metres on a clear, sunny day. It was frighteningly cold as he bit into a Snickers bar to gather strength for the onward journey. Except two other backpackers, there was not a single soul around.

Born in Kochi to a Tamil mother and a Gujarati father, Tejas spent his childhood in Mumbai. A life of frugality was internalised as he watched his parents work hard to provide a quality convent education to him and his brother. Throughout schooling and college, he avoided taking special coaching lessons and would depend on textbooks for his study. With a deep passion for studying abroad and getting into academia in computer science, Tejas picked

Canada. The US was too expensive. Soon, he was headed to Concordia University in Montreal, where he received a scholarship to pursue his master's degree.

The day would begin with working as a dishwasher at a local Italian restaurant, followed by a delicious salad lunch at the same place. Classes/research work would begin at 2 PM and go on until 7 PM. He taught a few undergrad students for a couple of hours after this. At the end of two years, he pitched for a thesis presentation on breaking the de facto popular AES cryptographic algorithm with means that were never thought through before. His professor, Dr Mourad Debbabi, the world-renowned data security expert, offered him a PhD option since he had cleared his thesis with honours.

However, Tejas had different plans.

Canada was an amazing place to live in, but entrepreneurship, start-ups and India beckoned. After a short stint at TCS to pay off his student loan, and also get some perspective on how corporates operated, Tejas found the perfect start-up to begin his entrepreneurial journey—Hidden Reflex.

Hidden Reflex was housed in a small home-office in the calm residential neighbourhood of J.P. Nagar, an old suburb of Bengaluru. Alok Bhardwaj, the founder, handled Sales, Marketing and Product, while Tejas handled Technology. They would work together for days on end, building a product that they believed would change the way people shared information. It was the time of social media. Orkut and Facebook were being talked about. Reddit was a goldmine of information. It was the best of times. Tejas rented a small room a kilometre away, lived by himself and cycled all around the city when free. Late-night technical brainstorming, working on beanbags and binging on art movies—it was Nirvana. Hidden Reflex, and the browser they had developed for the Indian audience, Epic, received rave reviews. At its peak it had 50,000 users.

A year had passed, but fundraising continued to be a challenge. His personal savings were depleting. Frustration had set in and Tejas was burning out rapidly. Sleep cycles were arrhythmic and there was also his then girlfriend, and would-be wife, Anitha's foreboding that this start-up wasn't going anywhere.

He left Hidden Reflex in August 2011 with a heavy heart after four really long years. Failure was written all over him. He felt distraught and lost. Low on self-esteem and feeling defeated, he packed his backpack with all that he could find and took the train to Gorakhpur, Uttar Pradesh, to enter Nepal. He hailed a bus, and with a *Lonely Planet* guide in his hand he landed in Jira, a small town in Nepal, at the base of the Himalayan forests to take the century-old trail to the Everest Base Camp and the 3 Passes trek.

He slept in monasteries and wayside wooden huts, mingled with local kids and encountered some near-death situations. The mind-numbing moment came atop the Kongma La with Everest far in the distance. This was one of the toughest passes in the world.

The 45-day solo trek in the Everest region was to change Tejas's life forever. He realised that tough times don't outlast tough people! Overcoming the bitterness and disappointment with the failure of his start-up, he decided to make a fresh beginning with a positive outlook.

The Decision to Join Bigbasket

It was a quiet afternoon in Domlur on a gloomy Monday. He remembers the date. It was 30 January 2012. He was a freelance consultant at Edgemetric and was also working on a new approach to getting meaningful insights by crunching terabytes of data.

An email popped up from a recruiter. Bigbasket was looking for a software developer and architect.

After three rounds of interviews, including one each by Abhinay and Sudhakar, he was offered the job. Tejas decided to take it. The interview process had convinced him that Bigbasket would be a good place for him. He joined on 27 February 2012.

Stress under Scale

On 7 June 2014, Pramod called Tejas to his cabin and asked him to look at some performance abnormalities that had hit the Bigbasket website.

Pramod had joined Bigbasket as the CTO in April and was also overseeing Product. The size of the Engineering team was seven. The business was growing by over 15 per cent month on month in Bengaluru. New features on the products, both front end and back end, were being released at a scorching pace. Deployments would happen every two days. Business would come up with an idea in the morning, the architecture and coding would be completed by evening, and deployment would happen the next day after a QA check.

This was the process. The systems had behaved well so far. However, of late, the systems had shown signs of stress. The website had begun to slow down. Open-source frameworks which enabled rapid development and prototyping could potentially affect performance if left unchecked.

The Bigbasket technology architecture had developed as a complex monolith. Performance issues with the front end could often be tracked (after hours of deep diagnosis) to some problem at the back end. Technology debt had been piling up. In the interest of speed, the quality of architecture had suffered. The quality of documentation was just as bad. When an engineer quit, there was no way to understand why something was architected or configured the way it was. One could not be sure what all would be affected if you tweaked a particular part of the monolith.

For the next two weeks, the seven engineering samurai got under the skin of every module and cleaned it up bit by bit. On 20 June, the odometer across every module showed a great spike in improvement. But this was still just another well-thought-out and clever band-aid.

It needed Rakshit to bring an outside-in perspective along with design thinking capability to nail the problem of scale.

Time to Take Stock of the Technical Debt

While Rakshit was winding down his start-up, he began to plan the next steps in his career. He had an offer from Google that would require him to move back to the US. It was a tempting offer from a professional perspective, but uprooting and moving his family again was not something he was keen to do. Around this time, he discovered the opportunity at Bigbasket through an executive recruiter. It was a bit surprising that despite being neighbours in the same community in Bengaluru, Rakshit and Pramod hadn't connected directly.

After the meetings with Pramod, Sudhakar and T.N. Hari, Bigbasket made Rakshit an offer. It was decision time. The opportunity at Google was exciting, but the chance to do path-breaking work at Bigbasket seemed more stimulating. Rakshit realised he had never worked for a B2C company like Bigbasket. It presented an opportunity for learning, but was also a significant risk because it was a new territory for him in terms of scale. The entrepreneur in him finally won and he accepted the offer from Bigbasket.

Rakshit came on board in March 2017 and quickly adapted to the frenetic pace of a growing Bigbasket. He liked the open and transparent culture, the absence of politicking and turf wars, and the speed of decision-making. He began to work closely with Pramod and offered suggestions for improvements to the engineering ecosystem at Bigbasket. His suggestions were driven by the best-in-class practices he had observed and adopted in his professional career before joining Bigbasket.

His initial observations formed the foundation for the next phase of building for scale:

- The start-up culture of everyone pitching in and doing anything that needed to be done had resulted in work being assigned based on bandwidth and not on expertise; this resulted in knowledge of any system being fragmented amongst team members.
- Code deployments took hours instead of minutes; processes were ad hoc and ownership was distributed.
- A centralised quality assurance team compromised ownership of quality.
- Lack of single ownership for IT infrastructure was affecting performance.
- There was no one to provide feedback and coaching every day for the engineers. In the absence of a process for continuously strengthening the tech competencies of engineers, the tech environment was not particularly invigorating or conducive for capability-building.
- Single code base and a monolithic database posed significant risk to scale and velocity of growth.

As Rakshit began working on solutions for these shortcomings, Pramod decided to go on a sabbatical. This occurred within three months of Rakshit joining Bigbasket. This was a big setback. Undeterred, Rakshit continued to work on implementing his recommendations, knowing that the pain felt in the short term would be offset by the significant benefits that Bigbasket would accrue in the long term.

He systematically drove initiatives that addressed all the gaps he had identified in his initial diagnosis:

- Separate teams for specific work areas were created and requests were assigned based on expertise and not availability of bandwidth. At times, this resulted in requests being delayed, waiting for the required expert to get free. But, this approach helped create a culture of prioritisation of requests instead of every request being worked on at the same time.
- Structured processes for code deployment and code freeze deadlines were adhered to, beyond which no change would be incorporated.
- Quality Assurance teams were embedded in the Development teams to establish accountability, ownership and maturity in development processes.
- A dedicated 'Platforms team' that would act as a single-point owner for the IT infrastructure was set up to deliver performance at scale.
- Engineering managers were hired to create the right technology capabilities and provide coaching to the developers.
- The architecture was reconfigured to a micro-services model. This helped compartmentalise the code base and isolate the risk of performance issues to the specific micro-service rather than the entire codebase and datastore.

Speed Versus Scalability

The biggest question that any start-up often faces is whether to invest time and effort upfront in designing a system that can scale effortlessly or build a product that would help you launch quickly and then make modifications along the way as the business scales. This is not a trade-off unique to either Bigbasket or start-ups in general. This is equally relevant in urban planning. We have all lived in cities where the here-and-now problem has been addressed but very soon serious problems begin to show up that need an open-heart surgery.

The need for rapid growth results in choices (people, process, architecture) being made based on the velocity needed to support growth while compromising on maintainability and scalability of the technology platforms. This results in the start-up acquiring 'technical debt' over a period of time. At some point, the burden of this technology begins to weigh heavily on performance and scalability. Organisations that pause to step back every couple of years to take stock of their technical debt, and work to retire the debt, thrive while those that don't do so, perish.

In Conclusion

The only constant in the technology industry is change.

—Marc Benioff

As Rakshit drove cultural, mindset and process changes at Bigbasket, he leaned on his past experiences implementing changes working with global teams made up of both seasoned as well as young members. He recognised that tech leaders like him, entering a rapidly growing but maturing start-up, face a unique challenge—earning the respect of the team they join. His advice for other leaders looking to make such a switch include being hands-on and building credibility with the team, getting to the details, and hiring leaders with a combination of experience and hands-on knowledge. These are traits of participative leaders in contrast to directional leaders. Leaders need to don both hats alternatingly over extended periods of time. Leaders who succeed are those who recognise which hat to wear in which situation. Directional leadership for a new leader could be a path to failure when she is new to the organisation, working to earn respect and credibility from the existing team. In contrast, participative leadership for a tenured leader could be a recipe for failure if the organisation is relying on her for providing strategic direction.

Bigbasket has entered a stage of maturity while continuing to grow at a fast clip. While the organisation is transforming from a nimble and lithe start-up to a large but mature one, leaders like Rakshit bring in the expertise needed to help manage this transformation in a way that does not compromise on growth while laying the groundwork for future scale.

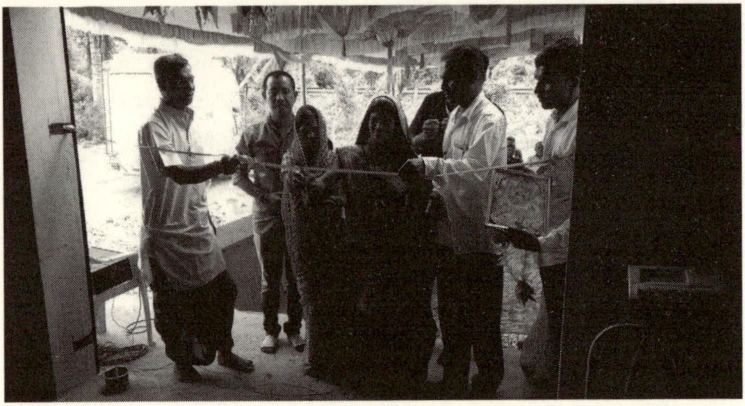

An F&V collection centre being inaugurated by the family members of one of our front-line staff

A POSH session in progress for the women packers at one of our distribution centres

At one of our leadership off-sites

Gopalakrishna receiving the Entrepreneur of the Year award in 2018

Inside one of our distribution centres

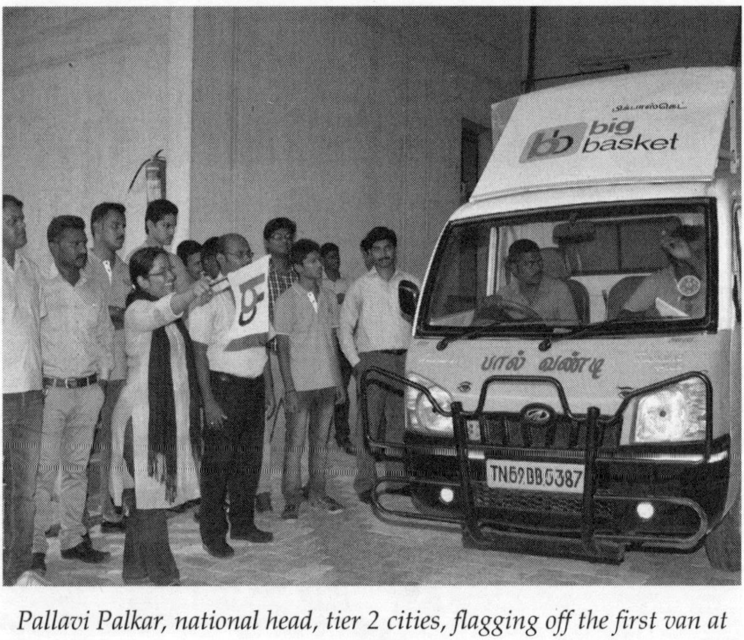

Pallavi Palkar, national head, tier 2 cities, flagging off the first van at Coimbatore

Regional business heads with the Rockstars

Some of our women leaders

Hari Menon (third from right) with the winners of the TRRAIN (Trust for Retailers and Retail Associates of India) award on either side of him.

Vans ready for departure from one of our transshipment hubs

A batch of differently abled people at Pune egging to go

Daily morning huddle also doubling up as reward and recognition for associates

Going green; doing deliveries using e-scooters

Monthly celebrations for our associates

The feisty VP(HR) of Bigbasket, Tanuja Tewari, with the region HR heads

With Bhuvaneshwari–Bigbasket's very own Shakuntala Devi

Women hired for warehouse jobs undergoing training

8
From POT to Ice Cream

Planning is everything. The plan is nothing.

—Dwight D. Eisenhower

For a business that delivers more than 2 million orders and 50 million items every month, across 22 cities and 150 facilities, planning is everything.

The supply chain needs to deliver a fill rate of 99.5 per cent, on-time delivery of 99 per cent and an out-of-stock experience of less than 1 per cent. This experience needs to be delivered every day, day after day. No e-commerce company in India has been anywhere close to achieving this kind of operating metrics so far. Grocery is time-sensitive unlike apparel or electronic goods. If a customer expects a delivery in the 7:30 PM to 10 PM slot, it is not acceptable to deliver the order before 7:30 PM or after 10 PM. Therefore, the logistics has to operate to clockwork precision irrespective of the traffic conditions. Nowadays, food delivery companies have mastered the art of express delivery, and food-tech has become the most time-sensitive e-commerce business.

Humble Beginnings

To get the business off the ground quickly, Bigbasket had started with an asset-light model by tying up with METRO Cash & Carry and Hypercity to fulfil orders. The founders were aware that this was just a stopgap arrangement and that sooner or later they would have to migrate to an inventory model. This happened in late 2012, about a year after launching operations on the back of METRO's inventory.

The first warehouse that Bigbasket took up was a small and dilapidated cement godown that was in disuse for some time at Mahadevpura, an industrial suburb of Bengaluru.

The godown was just 7,000 sq. ft in area. A cement factory was next door and if you parked your car outside for just 30 minutes, the windshield would be covered with fine cement dust. Srinath Reddy was the landlord. He wasn't sure how long Bigbasket would survive, but the founders seemed like good guys so he played along. He got involved in the construction of the warehouse and proved to be a long-term ally.

Part of the godown was used for warehousing FMCG products and the remaining area was used as a hub for 25 vans from where customer orders would be dispatched after segregation. For F&V, Bigbasket would continue to rely on the warehouse space of nearly 4,000 sq. ft that Safal had provided at Whitefield. A customer order could obviously comprise FMCG items as well as F&V. These two components of the order would come from different warehouses to the van hub where they would be assembled and segregated before dispatch.

As Bigbasket grew, the number of hubs (or transshipment points) in a city kept going up. Large trucks would first move orders in bulk from the warehouse to each hub, where they would be unloaded, segregated and re-loaded into smaller vans for final dispatch to customers. Over a period of time, there were a lot of small innovations in the movement from the warehouse to the hubs. Every link of the logistics chain had to be squeezed for efficiency.

V.S. Ramesh looked after warehouse operations initially. He studied the systems at a large offline retail company and found that the space utilisation of the trucks that moved goods from warehouses to their stores was as low as 40 per cent. He and his team worked on mechanisms to stack crates on pallets, used metal belts to clamp the crates together, and reengineered the mechanisms for loading these pallets onto the trucks. Soon, they achieved a utilisation of more than 90 per cent.

Very soon, the cement factory shut and the entire 30,000 sq. ft area was available. Bigbasket grabbed this opportunity and built a full-fledged warehouse with the first cold room and vacuum-dewatered flooring. The F&V warehouse at Safal was shut and moved here. When Krishnan Ganesh, one of the earliest investors at Bigbasket, saw this warehouse after it was fully built, his eyes popped out. Bigbasket would go on to build much bigger warehouses as business grew. A city like Bengaluru would soon have four warehouses, each four times the size of this first warehouse.

The Cold-Chain Conundrum

Bigbasket had taken a call from the beginning that, from a customer's perspective, it was important to not just provide dry grocery, but fruits and vegetables along with the chilled and frozen stuff. It didn't make any sense to have the customer visit a physical store for these items. In which case, the customer might as well buy dry grocery also from the physical store. Dry grocery was the easy part; everyone was doing it. The difficult and nearly impossible part was fruits, vegetables and the chilled and frozen stuff. Creating an end-to-end cold chain, which terminated at the customer's doorstep, had never been attempted before.

A customer order that was to be delivered in the morning hours would have been picked and packed in the warehouse the previous evening and moved to the transshipment hub at night. It would stay there overnight and be loaded into a van for delivery the next morning. The hub did not have any refrigeration equipment. So, if the order included chilled and frozen items, like leafy vegetables, frozen peas, butter or ice cream, these items would be lying at the hub overnight inside insulation boxes without active refrigeration. In all likelihood, from packing to delivery, it could take between 15–20 hours. Despite the best insulation boxes, the heat ingress would sometimes damage the products. Customer complaints were numerous for these categories.

There were additional complexities—leafy vegetables needed to be stored at a temperature of 5 degrees Celsius, meat at -5 degrees Celsius and frozen items like ice cream and frozen meats at -25 degrees Celsius. Any solution had to keep these nuances in mind.

The Innovations team worked hard on different solutions. They figured out that there had to be a way to either make the insulation boxes more effective and/or reduce the time from packing an order to transporting it to the customer's doorstep.

Soon, there was breakthrough on both the fronts. The Innovations team identified gels that would freeze at these three different temperatures. This gel was packed into hard plastic cases and frozen in different types of freezers at the warehouse. The team had to work with suppliers from across the world in fine-tuning and customising some of the designs. They tinkered with the insulation boxes by working closely with the manufactures in India and China. Very soon, there was substantial improvement in the ability of the boxes to prevent heat ingress. The chilled and frozen items were placed into insulation boxes along with a few of the frozen gel packs and locked. The latent heat of fusion of the gel was enough to keep the boxes cold for a sufficiently long period of time.

The other part of the solution, which was about reducing the transit time, aligned beautifully with a new customer requirement. It was about fulfilling small mid-month or mid-week top-up orders in express time. Bigbasket acquired Delyver to help build this business and this story will be told in the chapter titled 'Thoughtful about Build or Buy'.

The problem that Bigbasket sought to address through this was quick delivery of the most commonly consumed items. To do this, the inventory for these items had to be moved to customer clusters within the city and not held at a large and remote warehouse. These mini warehouses near customer clusters were called dark stores. The top-up and urgent orders of customers were directly picked from the closest dark store and a biker would take this order to the customer's doorstep within 60–120 minutes. The dark stores held between 2,000–3,000 SKUs as opposed to the 20,000 SKUs at the mother warehouse. They also had freezing equipment, and all items that needed to be supplied in chilled or frozen condition were stocked at the dark stores instead of at the mother warehouse.

Both these were breakthrough innovations in the cold chain.

The Big Leap

Given the positive effect on customer experience (faster delivery) and unit economics (delivery through bikes) of the express model, in mid-2016, Sudhakar and Gopala began planning the next big leap in Bigbasket's supply chain model. The project was code-named 5K, driven by the recognition that 80 per cent of sales came from an assortment of about 5,000 items (out of a range of over 20,000). So, there was a long tail of items that provided range to customers but contributed to only a small portion of sales. The 5K model centred on large dark-stores, which would hold a larger assortment (5,000–7,000) of items and would deliver to customers using a mix of vans and bikes. These 5K dark-stores were bigger than the earlier express dark-stores and were architected differently to handle different types of vehicular movement. This model delivered the best of both worlds (express and reasonably wide range). Customers could get all that they needed delivered in a single order within 4–6 hours for their planned purchases and get top-up needs delivered within 2–3 hours. As partners in crime, Sudhakar and Gopala continuously iterated with various levers of the 5K model, namely assortment in the dark stores, van-bike mix and location of the 5K dark-store, to deliver on the twin objectives of customer experience and unit economics. Over the last two years, Gopala and his team have worked tirelessly to deliver the metrics linked to these two objectives.

Bigbasket had two delivery models until now, namely the full-service model that serviced planned purchases and express model that serviced the top-up requirements. Now, both these models merged into 5K. Everything would be 'express' going forward, including large planned purchases. The switchover was an extremely tricky process because it could create huge disruptions if not planned well. The rollover to 5K was done store by store and not the entire city at one go, to minimise the risk of disruption or breakdown. It was like changing engines mid-flight as Vishal Gupta of Bessemer, a Bigbasket Board member, would remark.

Culture of Continuous Improvement

The individual who drives the supply chain nationally, with a strong team of process-oriented professionals, has earned his place in the league of superheroes at Bigbasket as the 'Supply Chain Man'. Gopala, the Supply Chain Man, who we met earlier in this book, lives and breathes planning, processes and metrics. His calm demeanour belies his laser-sharp focus, his no-nonsense attitude and his dedication to customer delight.

For someone who had managed warehouse operations in a 2,00,000 sq. ft facility at his previous job, joining Bigbasket to manage operations of a 7,000 sq. ft facility sounded like a big leap of faith from a career perspective. Moving from a well-established modern trade organisation to a fledgling start-up and making it a success story is the stuff of legends. Little did Gopala know when he joined Bigbasket that he was destined for such success. People at Bigbasket will have noticed the tag team of Sudhakar-Gopala constantly tinkering, iterating and reworking supply chain operations to deliver better efficiencies and lower costs. Therefore, it does come as a surprise that Gopala, whose every living moment at Bigbasket was inextricably linked to Sudhakar, neither interviewed with Sudhakar before he joined Bigbasket nor met him until after his first 50 days in the organisation.

The Early Challenges

Preparing Bigbasket to launch its inventory-led model with little or no impact on customers was the first challenge for the Gopala-Sudhakar duo. This was the first of the many wicked problems that Gopala would take on and solve with aplomb year after year.

After the switchover to the inventory model, Hari Menon pointed out to Gopala that the fill rate had dropped to nearly 95 per cent. While in most other organisation, this drop (99 per cent to 95 per cent) may have just caused a slight flutter, for a customer-obsessed organisation like Bigbasket, this fall was cataclysmic. A deep dive into the problem identified the 'planogram' as the culprit.

Planogram is an innocuous term for those who may not be familiar with the world of retail. You can be pardoned if you believed it was a metric weight measure like gram and kilogram. However, for someone living and breathing warehouse operations, planogram is a silent killer if designed incorrectly. A planogram is a diagram or plan that illustrates the arrangement of products in shelves to maximise operational efficiency. A well-designed planogram goes a long way in improving the efficiency of people who pick items from shelves just as a poorly-designed planogram could doom operational efficiencies. Planogram is like cholesterol—there are good planograms and bad planograms, and a bad planogram is a silent killer.

So, how did planogram affect the customer fill rate? Fill rates are typically pulled down either when items are not available to pick (availability issues) or when items are hard to pick (planogram issues). Gopala's investigation showed that in this instance, the cause was the latter.

Sudhakar and Abhinay got their hands dirty every evening after work hours along with Gopala, iterating on the planogram until they arrived at a design that guaranteed over 99 per cent fill rate.

To this day, Gopala and team follow some of the rules that were established then and revise planograms across all facilities every quarter. The rules were simple and straight:

- Ensure fast-moving SKUs (items) are closer to the near end of the starting point of picking action—pickers should be spending minimum time picking 80 per cent of the SKUs.
- Place two fast-moving SKUs slightly away from each other—you don't want a traffic jam amongst the pickers in the aisles.
- Push heavy SKUs to the bottom of the rack—avoid toppling of the racks.
- Segregate hazardous and non-hazardous SKUs—nobody wants to see biscuits being picked from the place next to toilet cleaners.

- Place products of the same brand away from each other—avoid mixing up Maggi chicken masala noodles with Maggi veg atta noodles.
- Keep SKUs of the same colour away from each other—ensure soap with a green wrapper is not mixed up with a packet of cloves of the same colour.

While these rules may appear to be plain common sense, as Voltaire once said, 'Common sense is uncommon.'

The Vendor Versus Partner Conundrum

The second big challenge that Gopala handled was a lesson in how Bigbasket treats those who are not its employees. Horror stories abound in the start-up world and in the corporate world of how contract employees, vendors, suppliers and others are treated by organisations.

Buddha said that everything is in the mind. There is no better illustration of this thinking than the example of how Gopala and team managed the thorny issue of suppliers and their timings. Gopala's supply chain ecosystem co-exists with the ecosystems of other teams, including Merchandising and Operations, among others. A new challenge that began to affect the availability of items was the arrival times of supplier vehicles that would bring in stocks to replenish inventory.

In the initial days of operations in the new warehouse, supplier vehicles would arrive at the warehouse any time of the day. At times, this resulted in confusion and chaos for the Bigbasket 'receiving' teams as well as for the suppliers. Receiving activities took longer than planned with significantly longer wait times for suppliers. In addition, items not being received in a timely manner affected inventory levels that impacted customer experience. The domino effect strained relations between the suppliers, the Bigbasket Supply Chain and Merchandising teams. Hari Menon's note to Gopala and Sundar (then head of merchandising) to fix this issue was a wake-up call.

Gopala and team sat down to solve the problem by applying first principles:

- Treat suppliers/vendors as partners. Recognising this as a mindset change, Gopala encouraged his team to work with suppliers to collaboratively solve challenges.
- Provide scheduled slots for suppliers to deliver materials—visibility to delivery slots allowed suppliers to plan their arrivals; this reduced chaos at the receiving stations.
- Set up fast-track receiving for small vendors—guarantee receiving to be completed within 60 minutes; this allowed small vendors to reuse their vehicles for delivery to other customers.
- Establish turnaround time (TAT) for large vendors—ensure receiving is completed within three hours.
- Set up waiting facilities for vendors—these facilities allowed drivers and other personnel from vendor teams to relax until receiving process was completed.
- Gather feedback for constant improvement—use feedback from vendors to resolve pain points.

Putting yourself in another's shoes was extended beyond just customers to all partners, including employees, vendors, contractors and other stakeholders.

Never a Dull Moment

As Peter Drucker had once pointed out, 'What is not measured cannot be improved.' With some basic principles set in place, the Supply Chain team began to focus on establishing metrics to allow review and improvement of warehouse operations. The team's goals were to deliver best-in-class metrics in process compliance, process improvements and inventory management.

Growth brings with it the pangs of expansion at a rapid pace. The expansion at Bigbasket was frenetic from 2015 onwards. Business expanded into new cities (tier 1 and tier 2) and into new business lines (express, speciality marketplace, kirana and HORECA [Hotel/Restaurant/Catering]). The Supply Chain team had to scale with a central team and regional teams in each city to roll out established processes across new facilities.

In Conclusion

'It is not the organisations that are competing. It is the supply chains that are competing,' said a supply chain leader in Europe. In grocery delivery, and particularly online grocery delivery, the events of 2015–16 have clearly demonstrated that the business model that is scalable and profitable in the long term is the model that relies on owning, or at least controlling, the supply chain. Bigbasket's business model holds promise because of the strong foundation of supply chain on which it is built. Bigbasket's customers order over 50 million items every month. To consistently deliver a 99.5 per cent fill rate and in-stock experience for its customers requires an extraordinary focus on supply chain.

Bigbasket's focus on building its back-end supply chain by setting up scalable processes, hiring the right talent without necessarily focusing on their educational pedigree and deploying technology to automate its processes in its initial years is beginning to pay off as the business grows two- or threefold year over year. Bigbasket continues to rely on large blue-collar workforces who are equipped with the right devices and tools to deliver an outstanding operational performance. The organisation's philosophy has relied on using technology where it best delivers value and not just because it is cool to use technology. The road ahead for Bigbasket's supply chain includes deploying advanced technologies such as the Internet of things, robotics-based picking and computer-vision aided item segregation with the key objective of delivering a superior customer experience and improving cost efficiencies.

9
Thoughtful about Build or Buy

More value is destroyed by acquisitions than any other single action taken by companies.

—Aswath Damodaran

Of all corporate actions, mergers and acquisitions (M&A) has always attracted maximum media attention and visibility. With funding opening up, some of the start-ups were attracting tonnes of capital well beyond what they needed to build their businesses organically. So, for the first time, we were witnessing a spate of M&As where both the acquiring and the acquired companies were start-ups.

'Synergy' is the most widely used and misused rationale in mergers and acquisitions. Author Aswath Damodaran has observed, 'Synergy is seldom delivered in acquisitions because it is incorrectly valued, inadequately planned for and much more difficult to create in practice than it is to compute on paper.'

To this we would like to add that when you are sitting on a large pile of cash, irrespective of whether you are a private or a public company, you begin to hallucinate synergies that do not exist.

Synergies can be either 'operating' or 'financial'. TaxiForSure's merger with Ola was a case of operating synergy where the combined cash burn was expected to come down significantly because of pricing power. Financial synergies can arise when there are legitimate tax benefits by using the acquired company's operating losses to shield income or simply increase the debt capacity or reduce the cost of capital.

Unless an M&A is planned and executed very thoughtfully, synergies are unlikely to be realised. In most cases, an acquisition is not worth the time, effort and cost.

Bigbasket has always viewed M&A through an interesting lens:

- Entrepreneurs are generally better at creating new businesses than managers. Ben Horowitz of Andreessen-Horowitz had once made an observation that contrasted a founder CEO from a professional CEO. We believe this can be extended to contrast entrepreneurs and managers. Entrepreneurs are generally better off than managers at *finding* product cycles, while managers are generally better off than entrepreneurs at *optimising* product cycles. For a start-up to continue the cycle of innovation-maturity-innovation, it is important to continue to acquire new founders who can add to the entrepreneurial horsepower and discover new product cycles. Therefore, an acquisition is about acquiring entrepreneurs as much as acquiring a business, and therefore culture fit and founder chemistry is very important. At Bigbasket, entrepreneurs who came in through acquisitions were welcomed, embraced, empowered and unleashed.
- Make an acquisition only if it helps you acquire market entry and/or some really new capability quickly. When it comes to building something versus buying it, the trade-off is about speed-to-market versus the risk of a failed acquisition.

In its seven years of existence, many acquisition opportunities came Bigbasket's way. At an anecdotal level, many of them would have passed the 'synergy' test.

However, under sharper scrutiny, only four of them truly fit all the criteria. All four were acquired, and it would not be an exaggeration to say that each of them lifted Bigbasket into successively higher orbits.

Acquiring Three Intrepid Founders

Bigbasket had modelled its business to mirror customer behaviour in an offline world for a long time. In an offline world, customers bought their planned monthly grocery at the beginning of the month. They also bought top-up and unplanned requirements a couple of times in a month. Fruits and vegetables were bought several times during the course of the month.

Bigbasket launched service with a model that addressed the planned monthly purchase. The average order size would be in the range of ₹1,200–1,500. The margin from such an order was enough to pay for delivering the order in a van and still leaving sufficient to cover the other costs. The rest of the cases did not make economic sense. For instance, the value of a top-up order mid-week or mid-month could be as low as ₹500. The margin from an order of this size was just about sufficient to cover the delivery cost, and hence not sustainable on a stand-alone basis. Therefore, for a long time, Bigbasket continued to focus on the planned monthly purchases with high Average Basket Value (ABV).

About the same time, there were a bunch of start-ups sprouting in the hyper-local space. It was becoming increasingly clear that the delivery model pioneered by such start-ups like Delyver, using two-wheelers, was more economical than deliveries made through four-wheelers. This suddenly made the lower value mid-month top-up grocery orders of customers worth looking at.

Many of the other grocery start-ups were using a marketplace model, however ineffective it may have been in totality, to provide express deliveries. This seemed to be a genuine customer need, and Bigbasket had to find an answer soon.

Sometime in October 2015, Bigbasket acquired Delyver, India's first hyper-local business. This was Bigbasket's first acquisition. The three founders of Delyver, Afsal Salu, Praful Thachery and Reebu Verghese, were the real assets that Bigbasket acquired. Delyver had a capability that Bigbasket did not have, namely doing deliveries through an army of bikers. Krishnan Ganesh of GrowthStory was a common investor and Sudhakar had been mentoring the Delyver founders. Therefore, the closure was achieved quickly.

Afsal Salu helped Bigbasket build out the express business.

The Delyver Story

After the acquisition by Bigbasket, when YourStory asked the unassuming founders of Delyver if they would have done things differently with the benefit of hindsight, this is what Afsal and Praful had to say, 'We don't have any regrets as such because the experience of starting Delyver was a huge learning experience for all of us. But, if it was at all possible, we would have timed our entry into this field differently. We were ahead of the curve and could not scale the business for the first four years or so. I believe that fast growth and a good team are essential for success in this space, and both require large amount of funds. That said, we're happy that in these five years we took care of all our stakeholders—employees, investors and customers.'

Almost immediately after the acquisition was announced, I (Hari) visited the Delyver office in Bengaluru, located off Sarjapura Road, to meet the extended team. Unsurprisingly, the office get-up was austere. The only wall hangings that passed off as any ornamentation were a series of simple

A4 size posters highlighting market innovations and business models pioneered by Delyver in India: 'First hyper local commerce platform in India for on-demand home delivery', 'First aggregator of home cooked meals under the Home Chef(s) programme', 'First to remove minimum order value in home delivery in India'.

The posters told a story that the self-effacing founders of Delyver were reluctant to talk about. The company was indeed a first mover in many of today's hottest segments several years before these segments even had names—hyper-local commerce, food tech, on-demand food delivery and the inventory-free, marketplace model.

In the interview with YourStory, Praful said half in jest and half seriously, 'In fact, we believe that we may have been the first to actually use the term "hyper-local" in the context of delivering food from local restaurants. We were struggling to describe to potential investors what Delyver did and found this word in a study done by some US university and used it. We later found that the term had become the buzzword to describe this type of business.'

In the same interview, Afsal said, 'Since we had no precedent before us, we had to figure out things as we went along. For instance, in 2011 there were no suitable options available in the market for the packaging of home chefs' food and delivery bags that kept the food warm. Therefore, the three of us sat together and designed food containers and delivery bags from scratch. We took the specs to a manufacturer and placed an order. The same manufacturer supplies containers that we designed to many of the late entrants.'

He went on to say, 'We built our early relationships with restaurants by making cold calls to ask if they were interested in letting us handle home delivery for them. As there was no listing fee, and payment was commission-based and not lead-based (that is, we got paid only for the orders that we delivered), most restaurant owners saw it as a no-risk proposition and signed up with us. Convincing customers to order through Delyver was a different ball game. Many customers were not used to the concept of home delivery and Delyver needed to win their trust by proving to them that its service was reliable.'

Their best advertising was the word-of-mouth reputation they had built for on-time delivery.

The Delyver founders were way ahead of their time and hyper-local was still not the 'in-thing'. Very soon though, after Delyver's acquisition, hyper-local began catching up and some new start-ups like Swiggy and Zomato began growing gangbusters.

After the acquisition, Afsal drove Bigbasket's foray into express delivery; Reebu helped build a marketplace of specialty stores; and Praful took on the responsibility of taking innovation to the next level. Their youth and enterprise gave Bigbasket a shot in the arm.

The Delyver founders also had the foresight to figure out that 'subscription' would be the next big thing. However, they were again a little ahead of time and weren't able to convince the rest of the management team. The reasons were straightforward—Bigbasket came from the ABV and margin paradigm. Here, unless the ABV was large enough, the margin was not sufficient to cover the delivery cost and hence the business would be inherently unsustainable. And orders based on subscriptions were bound to have low ABVs. The other belief was that grocery is inherently not a subscription business. So, the idea of subscription lay dormant for a long time.

However, in the meantime, new and more nimble start-ups had begun to redraw the boundaries in the subscription space and had also begun to receive funding from VCs who had spotted an opportunity. These start-ups were employing a different delivery model. This model was neither new nor innovative. Every small entrepreneur who delivered milk or newspapers had been using this. This had been referred to as the 'milk run' in the logistics industry. All the orders were bunched together and delivered early in the morning. Delivery cost per order was low.

These new start-ups were witnessing rapid growth. Along with milk, they made available a few other commonly consumed items like bread, butter, fruits and vegetables that customers could order along with the milk. The opportunity for Bigbasket was huge. Besides being a stand-alone business in its own right, subscription could also be a way to attract customers to the rest of the Bigbasket services. If Bigbasket executed well, the synergies would be quite strong.

The question again was, 'build' or 'buy'. Given the success with Delyver in building the express business, it was natural that 'buy' would be a serious choice. So, the search for potential start-ups in this space started in full earnest. One of the learnings from the Delyver acquisition was that magic could be created if there was a good culture fit. There were conversations with every single start-up in this space. Praful and Reebu led these conversations.

Finally Bigbasket zeroed in on 'Morning Cart' and 'RainCan'.

RainCan and Morning Cart

There are two things nearly every household in India is used to being delivered at their doorstep every morning, namely milk and the daily newspaper. One reason the print media, and particularly the daily newspaper, continues to thrive in India despite the onslaught of online media is the ready availability every morning. In most of the western world, home delivery of newspaper disappeared a while ago, laying the foundation for the dominance of online news media.

What about last-minute requirements beyond milk and the newspaper? Let's assume you realise late at night that the vegetables you need for the next morning have run out, or your child tells you just before going to bed that she needs some stationery for school next morning, or that you'd like tender coconut and bread also delivered in the morning, along with the milk.

What if you could do all this with just a simple tap of a button? That's exactly what Morning Cart, founded by Satish Shetty and Anuj Bishnoi, does. And that is what RainCan, founded by Abhijeet Kumar and Munendra Singh, also does. Morning Cart started in Bengaluru, while RainCan in Pune.

Abhijeet and Munendra were both from the 2005 batch at IIT Mumbai. They had worked together on multiple ideas before deciding to start RainCan. They ran an agro-based venture in 2010 where they grew exotic vegetables and cut-flowers in greenhouses. This experience helped them gain an understanding of the retail supply chain, especially for perishables.

The idea of Morning Cart was born when the milkman in Satish's society in Bengaluru stopped delivery, as he could not sustain collection of money and issuance of milk coupons. In another case, the milkman delivering to one of their friends' apartment complex disappeared after collecting an advance amount of ₹5 lakh from the residents.

This made them realise the need for a platform to organise this space. They began meeting and speaking with milk and newspaper distributors across the city. 'We concluded that there is a strong supply chain in the city that reached every home every day, but the distribution is unorganised and hence Morning Cart,' says Anuj.

Savis Retail

The fourth company Bigbasket acquired was Savis Retail. Founded by Neeraj Ray and Sameer Duggal, it operates cloud-connected, unmanned, smart vending machines under the name 'Kwik24'. With Kwik24, Bigbasket has so far installed 200 such machines across Bengaluru and plans to expand to other cities very soon. The vending machines are installed as part of the 'BB Instant' service. Customers can order fresh produce like fruits and vegetables and other FMCG products via the BB Instant app, and then pick it up from the vending machine.

The Kwik24 acquisition gave Bigbasket the ability to be closer to the customer by way of the BB Instant smart vending kiosks where customers can almost instantly gratify their need or cravings for items like cut fruits, noodles, juices, buttermilk or flavoured yogurt, and what makes it interesting is that these machines are 100 per cent unmanned and are operated only by our customers.

Praful and Reebu work very closely with the founders of Morning Cart, RainCan and Savis. Together, they are building the BB Daily and the BB Instant businesses. The collective entrepreneurial energy of seven founders, all of whom have come to Bigbasket through acquisitions, is quite amazing.

Beauty Business: Build, Not Buy

Sometime in mid-2018, when Bigbasket was evaluating adjacent businesses or categories where there could be some synergies, the one that bubbled to the top was 'Beauty'.

While Bigbasket carried some of the basic health and hygiene products, it had chosen not to carry the entire range of what constituted as beauty.

The obvious debate was whether customers who cared about beauty products would buy them from a company whose dominant business was grocery. Would a grocery company understand beauty well enough? Would it be seen cool to shop for beauty products at a grocery store?

Bigbasket handled several categories and each was remarkably different from the other. Gourmet was different from FMCG. Staples was different from meat. Fruits and vegetables were different from beverages. Therefore, it was just about hiring category heads, and teams, with expertise in these categories. Beauty was a different category and Bigbasket already carried close to 7,000 SKUs. Going the whole hog into beauty meant expanding this assortment to 30,000.

There were several good synergies as well. Bigbasket understood logistics, both national shipping as well as last-mile logistics. Bigbasket also understood warehousing, storage, inventory management, fill rates and assortment, among other things.

The thought that someone would not want to buy beauty products from an online grocery store was too flimsy and unsubstantiated to ignore these synergies. In the context of a physical store, customers for beauty products were more likely to visit a speciality beauty store as opposed to visiting the beauty section in a grocery retail for obvious reasons of ambience. However, this would be unlikely to reflect in online buying where the ambience does not matter as much. And creating a store-in-store experience online was so much easier.

Finally, why would a grocery customer not want to order beauty products through Bigbasket if she got an identical if not, superior assortment with a better delivery experience?

So, that's how Bigbasket launched its beauty business. There was no question of an acquisition. The internal synergies were strong and existing capabilities could be leveraged. It was just like adding a new category. A large warehouse in Mumbai was built to hold the entire assortment of 30,000 SKUs. This mother warehouse fed the regional warehouses, which held a smaller assortment of around 8,000 SKUs. Orders for any of the remaining SKUs were fulfilled by shipping the products on demand, from Mumbai to the regions where these orders originated.

This is just one of the many examples where Bigbasket chose to 'build' rather than 'buy'.

In Conclusion

Acquisitions rarely achieve the outcomes that they are meant to. However, when acquisitions are made thoughtfully, when the founders of the acquired companies are assimilated well, when they are made to feel at home, when they are supported with the capabilities of the acquiring company, and when they feel empowered, it can result in their entrepreneurial spirits being reignited.

In these rare cases, the proverbial synergies are realised and the outcomes are magical.

10
Mainstreaming Frugal Marketing

A salmon lays a million eggs but does so quietly; a hen lays a single egg and cackles a lot. Everyone eats hen's eggs; no one eats salmon eggs. Who said marketing and advertising don't work!

—***Anonymous***

Marketing at Bigbasket has always been frugal with the intent of getting bang for the buck. Vipul Parekh, one of the co-founders, heads the Marketing function and brings a wealth of knowledge acquired from his marketing experience in his prior stints. It is indeed a wonder that Vipul has any free time on his hands given that he dons multiple hats.

Vipul hired Pooja Ravishankar in 2013 to drive Marketing actions as Bigbasket began to grow rapidly. When Pooja came on board, Bigbasket had nearly 2 lakh customers and that number has now grown 50-fold. But, even in 2013, Bigbasket began to plan ways to grab the attention of its customers by personalising communication for them. The ball was set rolling with initiatives across various channels.

This is where the story of 'Frugal Marketing' at Bigbasket begins.

The Early Days: Try and Try until You Succeed

Marketing is too important to be left to the marketing department.

—David Packard

While David Packard said this in half jest, the truth about marketing, particularly in the world of e-commerce, is that an effective strategy is an outcome of how well various business teams come together to deliver on the promise of the organisation or brand. Marketing in Bigbasket was focused on achieving two key objectives, namely, getting the service right for its customers and scaling rapidly but with a measured approach. In line with these beliefs, the Marketing team leverages a host of channels to achieve its objectives. These channels include: a) search engine optimisation (SEO) for effective use of unpaid online visibility, b) search engine marketing (SEM) to squeeze the value out of paid marketing, c) outdoor opportunities such as hoardings, delivery van branding, bus shelters and more, d) print ads, e) radio ads, f) social media engagement and g) affiliates.

To this list of marketing armoury, Bigbasket added the powerful weapon of TV ads. Series B funding allowed Bigbasket to think big and to consider bringing on board a celebrity as brand ambassador. The choice was driven by the belief that the right brand ambassador could help Bigbasket get visibility in a market that was getting increasingly crowded, and provide credibility to the brand to help it achieve the next level of growth. More on this soon.

Marketing Aphorism #1: Define Your Brand

Up until 2015, Marketing at Bigbasket was driven by a mix of word-of-mouth, display ads at bus shelters, radio spots, some newspaper ads and—quite underrated—its delivery vans. With the exception of newspaper ads, the other channels were low-cost or no-cost, and succeeded in gradually building up scale. The delivery vans carried the Bigbasket logo and key aspects of its value proposition while traversing the city doing deliveries. This was a well-thought-out approach that leveraged the vehicle to act as a mobile advertising billboard. Besides just being an advertising platform, the vans also offered visibility and social proof of Bigbasket's service in action for existing customers and potential customers. It is no surprise that internal surveys done with customers indicate that vans have been a significant source of acquisition of new customers.

As the business scaled from the initial three cities in 2012 to over 25 cities in 2016, TV advertising started in September 2015. After deliberations, the leadership team chose Shah Rukh Khan as the brand ambassador. This choice was based on a very simple reasoning—Bigbasket wanted to be a brand for everyone. Shah Rukh Khan reflected that aspiration because he appealed to all segments of potential customers—from North to South India, from the young to the old, both men and women. His professional traits matched Bigbasket's values—he is known in the film industry for his professionalism and dedication to work. Shah Rukh has been the brand ambassador for over three years now. He has worked wonders for the brand and sales. One of the underrated, hard-to-quantify factors is the effect Shah Rukh has had on the spirits of everyone in the company—families, friends and neighbours of Bigbasket employees instantly recognise the brand now. It brings a sense of pride to delivery personnel and pickers as well.

The decision to go with Shah Rukh Khan was not totally uncontested though. There were those who felt a celebrity endorsement for grocery was not necessarily a great thing and could potentially backfire. There were some customers who wondered why we couldn't have been a little more creative in the way we positioned the company and service.

Every decision has its pros and cons. It is important to debate a point, take a decision and move on and that is what we did.

Marketing Aphorism #2: Spend Without Limits as Long as It Is Spent Frugally

In the early days, the focus of the Marketing team was to use suitable tools to develop a market for online groceries while persuading customers that Bigbasket was a service worth trying. The messages then were primarily about convenience and trust. Over the years, the messages have evolved to talk about the range of items available (e.g. household items, personal care, gourmet, etc.), helping Bigbasket transition to the position of 'India's largest online supermarket'.

For any online e-commerce business, digital marketing is a critical differentiator. On that front, until early 2015, Bigbasket had a presence on Google (SEO and SEM) and a small presence on Facebook. At that point, all digital marketing was directed towards Bigbasket's website given that nearly 90 per cent of revenue was coming from there. Over the next four years, the smartphone market in India exploded. Every household—rural and urban had a mobile phone and most of them also had a smartphone. With falling telecom prices, both for voice and data, the world of mobile applications (apps) suddenly emerged as the battleground for market share and mindshare of customers. Recognising the potential of apps, Bigbasket launched the first version of its app in 2014 but expanded rapidly with newer versions every few months. The launch of the app was so timely—in just about a year, the share of sales from the Bigbasket app grew to 70 per cent , while the share of sales from the website dropped from the highs of 90 per cent to just about 30 per cent.

It was not just Bigbasket that experienced this sudden but dramatic shift in share of revenue across website and apps. Many of the leading e-commerce brands in India also saw the same trend.

Some brands took a simplistic approach by using a linear extrapolation to estimate the share of business from the app vis-à-vis the Web, and concluded that in the next 12–18 months all users would shift to the app. Based on this mistaken conclusion, some of the big brands began to shut down their websites. Somehow, our intuition told us otherwise. We believed that there would always be customers who would be more comfortable, for a bunch of reasons, placing orders on the website. An app or a website is just a channel and we had seen that all predictions in the past about the imminent death of a channel always proved to be wrong. There was no reason to believe that this time would be any different.

Therefore, Bigbasket never discriminated (in the form of marketing spends, features and more) between the app and the Web. Looking back, this belief has been validated. However, during 2016, in all the madness that engulfed the market, it was a bold but risky move to maintain (and therefore spend on) multiple channels for customer engagement. With the rapid growth of mobile app usage, 'push notifications' became a big source of traffic.

Bigbasket also tried several new channels, some worked out and some didn't. Nevertheless, the Marketing teams continue to learn about this ever-growing medium of sales and customer engagement. One such channel whose ability to power sales was not well understood in the initial days was the affiliate and partner channel. Over the years, this channel has grown rapidly with an ever-improving range and depth of partnerships. For its partners, Bigbasket offers a repeat rate and customer engagement that is quite likely unmatched in the industry. Along the way, the Marketing team also added offerings like gift cards supported by partners and affiliates.

Marketing Aphorism # 3: The Powerful but Virtuous Cycle of Measure-Improve-Measure

Through all these changes, Bigbasket's marketing efforts have been grounded by a focus on metrics such as cost per acquisition (CPA) and quality of cohorts. Even as the business grew bigger, the Marketing team continued to focus on maintaining a reasonable cost per acquisition and healthy repeat rates. Also, the mantra that quality of service is the best form of advertising has informed everyone about the marketing efforts. Anyone who has been in the services industry, customer or enterprise, understands this well. Marketing efforts are aligned with the belief of the founders that a great customer experience is the foundation of the retail business.

Cross-Functional Efforts Paid Off

We soon realised that all complex problems, and certainly those in marketing, cut across multiple functions and it was important to drive solutions through cross-functional teams. We also discovered that one of the unintended consequences of a cross-functional effort was that it helped create terrific bonding, and even after the initiative was closed, the collaboration between teams on a day-to-day basis saw a huge uptick.

Here is one such example of cross-functional collaboration.

We noticed that conversion rates (which we define as customers/visitors to our app or website) had always been unusually high. In the initial days, this was partly because our traffic mix was largely organic. While the addition of paid marketing to the mix has, as expected, had a dampening effect, conversion rates have still been fairly good. That being said, we realised in early 2017 that we were receiving a lot of new visitor traffic, especially from the mobile website and Android app that resulted in a drop in conversion. We constituted a cross-functional team, comprising Vipul, Sudhakar and a few people from the Digital Marketing and Product teams to improve conversion. Several good things came out of this—a clearer definition and classification of conversion rates that made sense for Bigbasket, and a completely new checkout flow and simplified registration, among others.

The collaboration between the Marketing, Analytics and Product teams saw a marked improvement after the success of some of these cross-functional initiatives.

In Conclusion

Marketing at Bigbasket has always been aligned to the bigger goals. For example, we soon figured out that the Average Basket Value (ABV) was the biggest driver of profitability, or even sustainability, of the business. Let's just take a hypothetical example. If the ABV is ₹1,000 and the margin is 20 per cent, in absolute terms, the margin works out to ₹200. Let's further assume that all the costs, other than the cost of last mile delivery, is 12 per cent, or in this case ₹120. Then unless the last mile delivery cost per order is less than ₹80, there would be no way the business could break even. So, bringing down the cost of delivery and increasing the ABV was absolutely critical.

Everyone, including Marketing, had to align to this Holy Grail. Marketing could not drive initiatives that would drive down the ABV in the medium to long term though they had some leeway in the short term. While it was important to onboard trial customers who would be making first-time purchases with Bigbasket, often with low ABVs, it was important to drive campaigns that would slowly but surely push up the ABVs of subsequent orders.

Marketing spend can soon go out of hand if there is no serious focus on measuring returns. Most traditional marketers didn't necessarily understand how to measure the impact of marketing initiatives. However, in the last decade or so, marketing analytics has come of age and emerged as an important capability within marketing to assist people in making the right decisions. Our frugal marketing approach has been powered by our strength in marketing analytics from day one.

11
Show Me the Data

Without data, you're just another person with an opinion.
—W. Edwards Deming

Mrs Bhat[1] just finished placing her order on Bigbasket.com. With two teen kids in school and college, a husband whose work keeps him on the road four days a week and with a mushrooming interior decoration service, Mrs Bhat could do with any help she could receive in the kitchen. While she had a cook to assist her, Mrs Bhat had realised that the cook was not the one to rely on when it came to cutting vegetables in preparation for her recipes. Mrs Bhat's recipes were handed to her by her mother who had received them from her own mother. They were family treasures and Mrs Bhat took great pride in preparing dishes that adhered to the recipes in letter and spirit. No wonder her family adored her preparations.

The reason Mrs Bhat did not trust her cook's slicing and dicing of the vegetables was because her recipes required finely-cut vegetables, while the cook believed that how you sliced your vegetables had no impact on how well they got cooked. Over the years, Mrs Bhat had tried her best to get her cook to mend her ways but with little or no luck. So it fell on Mrs Bhat to prepare the vegetables the night before—day after day, year after year.

1 A fictional persona representative of our customers

Mrs Bhat chanced upon Bigbasket when a neighbour raved about the convenience, range and savings from ordering groceries. Mrs Bhat wasn't convinced that groceries could ever be bought online. However, she did realise that the 2–3 hours that she spent in a large format modern retail store near home every week and the 15–30 minutes that she spent at the nearby kirana store every 2–3 days could be best used elsewhere if only she could find a suitable alternative to these stores. So, when she kept hearing from neighbours about the reliability of Bigbasket, she decided to test the waters by placing an order of a small value of ₹1,001 (it was auspicious and also helped her get free delivery).

She was impressed when she learnt that she could pick the time and date of delivery. She picked a morning slot on Saturday, knowing that she'd be relatively free to check the items when they were delivered. Lo and behold, when the order was delivered, she was delighted by the fact that the executive who delivered the order spoke pleasantly, waited until Mrs Bhat was able to verify all the items and left within five minutes from the time of arrival. What used to take no less than two hours (even on a day with normal traffic) was done in 12 minutes (including the time to place an order). Mrs Bhat couldn't believe that she now got back two hours every week that could be put to better use.

Mrs Bhat soon moved from being an agnostic e-commerce customer to a delighted Bigbasket customer. She realised that the service from Bigbasket was convenient (saved her time), offered a great range (she was able to find products from her hometown that were featured in her granny's recipes) and was cheaper than her neighbourhood stores. She had come to trust Bigbasket so much that from ordering just staples she had moved to ordering fruits and vegetables. Not stopping there, she realised Bigbasket also offered cut vegetables. Her ongoing challenge of getting her cook to cut vegetables to her expectations ended the day she received her first order of cut vegetables. They were clean and cut to her exacting specifications.

Going back to the day when she had just finished placing her latest order with Bigbasket, imagine her surprise when she received a notification on the app telling her that if she was delighted by the quality of their cut vegetables (because they were a time-saver), why not try their shredded coconut? Not just that, she was offered a 20 per cent discount for her first order. Mrs Bhat added shredded coconut to her next order and was delighted by the quality of the product. Her surprise did not end there—she noticed that her smartbasket (a personalised shopping list feature on Bigbasket) recognised that she had started buying shredded coconut and had the item in the list when she was ready to place her next order.

This was a bit of a shocker for the mild-mannered Mrs Bhat. A bunch of questions began to swirl in her head. How did Bigbasket know that shredded coconut was another time-saver for her? How did they know that given her great experience with cut vegetables, she was just ready to try out shredded coconut? How did they know that at 20 per cent discount, the price was just right for her to give shredded coconut a try? And how did they know that she was going to need the item again and rightly placed the item in her smartbasket?

Later that evening when she was chatting with her daughter, she brought up these questions. Her daughter, who was preparing for a career in business, helped her understand that all the 'magic' that Mrs Bhat was experiencing was due to the power of Analytics that Bigbasket was leveraging to deliver customer delight.

This is where the story of Analytics at Bigbasket begins.

Analytics Version 1.0: Building the Foundation from $0 to $50 Million

In God we trust; all others must bring data.

—W. Edwards Deming

Bigbasket has a strong reputation in the e-commerce ecosystem of being a data-driven organisation. This reputation was built over many years because the founders believed it could be a strategic differentiator. This ethos, set in the early stages of the organisation, continues to drive all actions in the organisation even seven years after its foundation.

Among the many advantages that online retail firms enjoy over their offline counterparts, the advantage of data acts as a force multiplier. Imagine, an offline retail firm trying to understand: a) of all customers who came in, how many were new and how many were returning customers; b) customer conversion rates; c) customer experience at the store—which aisles did they navigate, what challenges did they face in buying items, what were speed breakers in their purchasing experience; d) what did they search for and what did they buy and not buy; e) what are their demographics and more. These are just some of the many aspects of shopping that online retail firms have rich data to understand customer behaviour and enhance their shopping experience. The Analytics ecosystem at Bigbasket from day one was designed to leverage this unique power of data to deliver a best-in-class experience for its customers.

In August 2013, Vipul Parekh hired Pooja to help manage some of the activities in the Marketing function. Pooja is a firm believer in data-driven marketing and so she began to focus on building a data repository that could drive more meaningful marketing actions. At that point, a rudimentary data warehouse was in existence and it hosted some datasets from the transaction system. Pooja's three-point plan in 2013 included building a robust data warehousing platform, deploying an impactful visualisation solution and leveraging a scalable customer engagement platform.

Pooja is a native of Bengaluru who completed her engineering degree in telecom. She finished her MBA education next. To this day, she keeps wondering if she could have gotten more out of her MBA had she worked for a few years after achieving her engineering degree. Pooja's initial days at Bigbasket were very similar to what anyone would experience when they join a start-up that is growing at a breathtaking pace. To Pooja, who relishes challenges and moving at breakneck speed, the Bigbasket opportunity seemed just like what the doctor ordered for her. In her first 12 months at Bigbasket, Pooja took on every single marketing project that Vipul threw at her—designing campaigns, planning offers, managing print and radio ads and more. Along the way, working with Sudhakar, she helped set up the foundation for an Analytics data warehouse.

Pooja never hesitates to call a spade a spade. In any discussion, regardless of the hierarchy of people participating in the discussion, Pooja cuts through the jargon and niceties to get to the core of the issue at hand. Putting herself in the shoes of a customer comes naturally to her and, therefore, her single-minded focus in any problem-solving situation is to do right by the customer. While trying to hire the first set of team members for the Analytics team, Pooja quickly realised that hiring for attitude and aptitude would be critical. The custodian of all data in the enterprise was the Analytics team. In many of the situations, where critical decisions had to be made using data, the leadership team and others in the organisation relied on the data provided by the Analytics team. Therefore, it was imperative that the team hired to manage the data warehouse demonstrated attention to detail, ownership and proactiveness. In her pursuit to hire the right kind of talent, Pooja hit on the idea of hiring fresh engineering graduates. It was easy to assess the attitude and aptitude of such graduates and they came with no professional baggage. These fresh grads also provided Pooja the opportunity to mold them into seasoned professionals from their very early days. This strategy has worked very well for the Analytics team over the years.

Analytics at Bigbasket has always been focused on leveraging data to deliver a fantastic customer experience, power growth in sales and drive reduction in costs. The Holy Grail in delivering a fantastic customer experience was the ability to develop segments of one. 'Segment of one' marketing is based on the principle of using data to establish a one-to-one relationship with a customer by treating him or her as unique and not as part of a large cohort. From its early days, Bigbasket focused on communicating with customers using emails and push notifications by creating segments of one. Bigbasket was a pioneer in thinking of and adopting this approach well before it became commonplace in 2015 and beyond. Another milestone at this stage was the fact that even before it became fashionable to build one's Analytics ecosystem on the cloud, Bigbasket's was birthed in the world of cloud services.

Bigbasket's operating philosophy has always been to be frugal but impactful in its investments. With that guiding principle, Bigbasket engaged with a set of partners to build its visualisation, customer engagement and warehousing platforms. There were mixed results—the partner who developed the visualisation platform became an extended team and provided a very cost-effective solution. Bigbasket stands out for being, maybe, the only large start-up to leverage a niche cost-effective visualisation solution and not any of the tools (such as PowerBI, Tableau and the likes) used by the rest of the industry. The customer engagement platform had a set of challenges that limited Bigbasket's ability to fully achieve its objectives. The data warehouse platform supported Bigbasket's initial growth phase, but began to sputter with growth pangs beyond a stage. In essence, outcomes from Bigbasket's version 1.0 of its Analytics platform were a mixed bag in terms of impact and results.

Analytics Version 2.0: Building for Growth from $50 Million to $250 Million

Subramanian (fondly referred to as Mani, and a co-author of this book) was hired to lead the Analytics team as Bigbasket began to fire all cylinders of growth. This phase of growth included expansion into tier 2 cities and of new lines of business, namely, express and specialty. Mani's interview with Sudhakar was marked by a debate on the relevance of Net Promoter Score (NPS) in India and if it really was a predictor of sales growth. NPS, when it was originally introduced in the world of business in 2003, was touted as the next big management tool to understand one's customers. Organisations were advised by hordes of management consultants to use NPS as the one number to track and to use it as a predictor of growth. In the last few years, experts have begun to question the belief that NPS is a predictor of growth. Some of the experts contend that NPS is at best just a substitute for customer satisfaction and no more than that.

At Bigbasket over the three years that NPS has consistently been measured, it has never had a strong correlation with the sales growth. During months when NPS has risen, sales growth has slowed down and vice versa. An emerging school of thought is that an organisation's NPS on its own is not a predictor of growth but that it should be read in conjunction with the NPS of the competitors to understand its relation to growth.

Version 2.0 of the Analytics ecosystem at Bigbasket was focused on achieving the following: scale the data warehouse platform to support the expected growth from $50 million to $250 million a year, deliver the dream of customer engagement by building segments of one and build a clickstream solution to help understand user experience. To achieve these objectives, the Analytics team made some strategic choices in terms of platforms, people and partners. One of the key platform choices was to use Snowplow Analytics as the tool for clickstream analysis. In doing so, Bigbasket again broke the mould by using an open-source, cost-effective, scalable and flexible choice rather than adopt the standard tools from Google and Adobe that other start-ups use by default. This bold bet has since paid off handsomely via the total cost of ownership, which is a fraction of what Bigbasket would have incurred if it had made one of the safer choices. The choice of Snowplow Analytics did have its risks (open source with limited support, limited availability of expertise and time to implement, to name a few) but with its trademark approach of keeping its nose to the grindstone, Bigbasket has managed to deploy the solution and reap significant benefits from the tool.

Version 2.0 of the Analytics ecosystem also marks the finalisation of key business metrics to understand customer segments (RFM) and sales performance (basket value, monthly customer value, frequency, to name a few). Establishing these metrics, defining them in a precise manner, tracking their performance consistently and aligning the organisation's focus on these metrics have helped Bigbasket scale the business nearly six times with a simultaneous improvement in many of these metrics. This contrasts with what usually happens in other organisations where such a growth in sales is accompanied by deterioration in some of the key business metrics.

Analytics Version 3.0: Building for Scale from $250 Million to $500 Million

As business began to grow rapidly, the Analytics ecosystem focused on achieving the following objectives: build a framework to analyse business performance and drive quick decisions to arrest decline or drive further growth as relevant, and deploy powerful analytical solutions such as recommendation systems, pricing solutions, shopping assistants, forecasting solutions and assortment planning to fuel growth efficiently.

A new term that entered the Analytics vocabulary in this phase is Definitive Actionable Insights (DAI). This key term symbolises Bigbasket's approach because it believes Analytics is a strategic differentiator, if and only if: a) analytics is about insights and not just data; b) insights need to be definitive, that is, non-arguable and conclusive; and c) they are actionable, that is, insights that can be executed.

All requests to the Analytics team are evaluated to ensure that they are driven by a hypothesis—to be proven or disproven and not just requests for data. The hypothesis driven problem-solving approach with the focus to deliver definitive, actionable insights has helped Bigbasket use Analytics as a strategic differentiator.

Some of the key challenges in Analytics version 3.0 were around communicating effectively to its customers the benefits of some of the features. For example, the feature of smartbasket is designed to minimise the time taken by customers to complete their order. Developed using a homegrown algorithm, the smartbasket helps a customer complete their shopping in seven minutes versus twice the time taken on average by a customer not using it. In addition, the smartbasket helps a customer avoid missing any item they are likely to need. A customer not using the smartbasket is likely to miss such items if they search or browse. Smartbasket is a unique feature personalised for every customer, built using their own shopping behaviour and computed every day for about 1.1 crore customers. It is a smart shopping list that reduces the hassles of grocery shopping. Customers who use smartbasket swear by its usefulness but the challenge that the Analytics team continues to face is to help its customers discover this feature. Feedback (first-hand and second-hand) from customers indicates that they'd like a feature such as smartbasket but haven't noticed that it already exists on the Bigbasket website and app.

Another challenge is getting customers to make the best use of recommendations generated for them. The recommendation feature is typically built to help customers discover products that they are likely to need but are unaware are available with Bigbasket. In the non-grocery retail world, customers usually do not buy the same products month after month and hence recommendation systems are critical to drive up order values by helping customers discover new products. In grocery retail, Bigbasket has observed that a large share of a customer's monthly purchases is repetitive (vegetables, fruits, oil, masalas, toothpastes). Just about 10 per cent of a customer's monthly purchase is made up of new items. While many in the Analytics world speak highly of the recommendation systems of Amazon and Netflix, the gold standard for recommendation systems is arguably Spotify's. Spotify is a digital musical service that smartly learns its user's preferences and generates recommendations that are absolutely adored by its users. The Internet is rife with proclamations from users who have believed that no human being understands them as well as Spotify does and there are many among those who would happily commit to a life with Spotify if it were a human! The goal for the Analytics team at Bigbasket is to enhance its recommendation system to the level where these systems understand the customers better than any human could ever do.

Version 3.0 of the Analytics ecosystem marks the deployment of Analytical models—recommendation systems, forecasting models, shopping assistants and more, at production scale for 1 crore or more users. The investments over the year to build a robust, scalable Analytics ecosystem are beginning to pay off now as the organisation begins to focus on the next phase of scale driven by growth.

Analytics Version 4.0: Building for Take-off from $500 Million to $1 Billion and Beyond

As Bigbasket gets ready to clock revenues of $500 million a year and aims to achieve $1 billion a year by 2020, the focus of the Analytics team is to build solutions that act as engines of growth for the existing and acquired business lines. The two key objectives to achieve in the next 6–12 months are: leverage advanced techniques, including deep-learning techniques, to solve the wicked problems of the grocery business; and replicate the Analytics platform of Bigbasket to the same degree of success in its acquisitions—BB Instant and BB Daily, to help deliver DAIs for these businesses as well.

Some of the problems in the grocery business that Analytics version 4.0 will try tackling include forecasting for perishable items such as fruits, vegetables, breads, etc., and improving customer perception of Bigbasket's fruits and vegetables.

Statisticians widely believe the axiom that all forecasts are wrong. To reduce the chance of error in a forecast, buffers are used to handle the variability that could cause errors. Using buffers in a forecast for say, a product like rice, works well because it ensures that an error due to under-predicting demand is mitigated. If the forecast error is due to over-predicting demand, the buffer quantity that becomes excess quantity could be carried over without any risk of wastage. This approach does not work well when applied to the universe of perishables. For perishables, buffer quantities help in case of under-prediction of demand but when they become excess due to over-prediction, they cannot be carried over to meet the demand for another day since perishables have short shelf life. In such a situation, the buffer quantity may have to be written off as wastage. Analytical models that try tackling this challenge of forecasting perishables focus on not necessarily maximising sales (by increasing buffer quantity) but minimising both out of stock and wastage situations. One of the key challenges that Analytics 4.0 at Bigbasket will tackle is to build a scalable solution that could deliver minimum out of stock and wastage. Truly a wicked problem!

Bigbasket strives hard to deliver best-in-class quality fruits and vegetables to its customers. However, there have been two key challenges in getting its customers to see Bigbasket as the destination for fruits and vegetables: perception that the quality is not up to their expectations and reality that in some cases the quality may actually be below customers' expectations. Solving both these challenges provides a great opportunity to apply data-driven DAI. To solve the issue of quality, either a manual but hard-to-scale solution could be used—have pickers manually select the right quality products—or build a scalable technology solution that could do as good a job as manual pickers in identifying right quality products. The technology solution provides a great opportunity to apply advanced analytical techniques such as deep learning. Bigbasket has always believed that leveraging technology just because it is cool does not provide sustainable advantage. Deep-learning, for all the hype around it, is fundamentally an approach to mine very large volume of data and detect patterns in them to decipher relationships. Deep-learning solutions continue to remain black boxes, thereby limiting the ability to draw conclusive relationships between input and output. A real example of a quandary this could pose to a business is illustrated by the situation where one of Bigbasket's customers reached out to the Analytics team to understand why a certain variety of mango was showing up in the customer's smartbasket. Because the smartbasket is built on a homegrown algorithm, the team was able to parse through the customer's data, analyse how the algorithm transformed the data that resulted in the specific type of mango finding a place in the customer's smartbasket and explain the outcome to the customer. A black box algorithm, on the other hand, could put the organisation in an awkward position while responding to the customer. What would the team provide as response to the customer—that they had no idea because the model said so? How awkward would that be?

In areas such as image and natural language processing, deep-learning technologies are beginning to demonstrate consistent and predictable impact. So using image processing to develop models that could distinguish between a good apple and a bad apple (literally not figuratively) could help Bigbasket significantly improve customer experience. Another of the wicked problems that could be solved with a data-driven approach.

As the book gets written, Bigbasket is embarking on version 4.0 of the Analytics ecosystem to leverage data/ advanced analytical techniques to drive deeper impact by tackling the wicked problems which, when solved, could become game changers in the grocery business.

In Conclusion

Information is the oil of the 21st century and analytics is the combustion engine.

—Peter Sondergaard

The belief that data/information is the new oil is an oft repeated expression to the point of becoming trite. The truth still is that organisations that learn to use data for competitive advantage are more likely to be leaders than those who don't. With this belief in mind, Bigbasket has, over the years, evolved its Analytics platform to help it develop strategic levers to maintain its leadership position in the grocery business.

What differentiates Analytics at Bigbasket from how others use it in the e-commerce retail business in India? For starters, Bigbasket does not rely on the fanciest and coolest tools for Analytics. Bigbasket's strategy to build or buy solutions that exactly meet its needs has worked well so far. This is exemplified by the tools/solutions in the Analytics ecosystem at bigbasket—no Google, no Adobe. Homegrown and open source solutions are the tools of choice. Second,

Analytics and data science solutions are not restricted to just the Analytics team within Bigbasket. Use of data to drive insights and application of Analytics and data science tools and techniques are commonplace in the organisation. Innovation, Category, Operations and Marketing teams partner with the in-house Analytics team or a suitable third-party partner to leverage Analytics to drive performance improvements. This has resulted in an ecosystem of partners that bring niche analytical expertise and rapidly deploy that expertise to solve pressing problems at scale. Lastly, the focus on Analytics and adoption of data-driven decision-making is driven top-down in the organisation, starting with the founders. The belief in Analytics as a strategic lever, driven from the top, has created a culture of hypothesis-driven problem-solving and DAI-based application of Analytics to overcome business challenges and to identify opportunities for growth.

12
Miserably Excellent No More

Quality is never an accident; it is always the result of high intention, sincere effort, intelligent direction and skillful execution; it represents the wise choice of many alternatives.

—***William A. Foster***

A consistently outstanding customer experience is often at the intersection of excellence in people, process and technology. Of all the three, the emphasis is a lot more on 'process' at Bigbasket. The belief is that even average people, if equipped with the right process and training, can deliver outstanding results.

There are broadly four components of customer experience in a Bigbasket context:

- The ease of placing an order on the app or website, which includes, among other things, discoverability, effectiveness of search, ease of navigation and the check-out process.
- The overall delivery experience, which includes timeliness, the behaviour of the delivery person and his ability to handle exceptions.
- The quality of assistance provided in resolving complaints.
- The quality of the products itself.

In this chapter, we will focus on how Bigbasket has dealt with the second and third aspects of customer experience.

Grocery Delivery Fundamentals

Let's step back for a moment and understand the criticality of delivery operations and process in the Bigbasket context. Delivery operations is really where the rubber hits the road. We do not have the luxury of calling up a customer at any time of the day to check if she's at home. We need to deliver the order in a predefined time slot chosen by the customer. That's not all. The order often comprises items of all shapes and sizes. And there are fragile items that need special care.

To illustrate the point, a single order could comprise FMCG items like a packet of Surf, frozen items like meats and ice cream, a toilet cleaner, fruits and vegetables, eggs, vegetable oil in plastic pouches, a broom and a weed trimmer. In this particular order, there are fragile items, food items, non-food items, frozen items, and items that can't be packed in a crate.

All of them need to be neatly packed and assembled to start with. The food items can't be mixed with the non-food items.

To top it, this order is not a doorstep delivery. The delivery person needs to enter the customer's home and neatly arrange the items on the table or at any other place indicated by the customer. The customer has to check and reconcile the items delivered against those shown in the invoice. If there was an exception like a missing or a damaged item, this needs to be addressed then and there by the delivery person. If the delivery person is unable to answer any question, he needs to call up Bigbasket customer service and take their help.

Bigbasket had consciously taken three difficult calls right from the beginning, namely: a) there would be a 'no questions asked' returns policy where a customer did not have to explain why she was unhappy with the quality of a product. If she was unhappy, the product could be returned and the money would be instantly refunded to the customer wallet, b) there was a delivery guarantee where if the delivery was delayed beyond the end of the time slot even by a minute, the customer was paid 10 per cent of the order value. Given the fact that the grocery business was a low-margin one, this was a huge self-imposed penalty, c) a delivery boy was not supposed to get in touch with the customer for last mile navigation or for any other reason. The delivery person had to take help from either the operations controller at the transshipment hub or an agent at customer service. The underlying reason was to control the quality of the interaction. If delegated to thousands of delivery persons on the ground, it would be impossible to control the quality of this conversation.

It was not without reason that the delivery person was designated as a Customer Experience Executive (CEE). He is assisted by a delivery app in which the orders, the expected time of arrival (ETA) for each order and order contents are all visible. He actually receives and updates money collected and even processes returns with instant wallet credit to the customer. In short, CEE is an empowered front-face to the customer. The CEE at Bigbasket is, therefore, well-trained in navigation, use of the app to handle transactions like returns, cash, as well as soft skills to behave courteously during the few minutes he spends inside a customer's home.

Planning Deliveries

Let's start with some basics on how the delivery to customers is planned and executed on the ground. When the customer places an order, she also chooses her preferred timeslot for delivery. Each delivery timeslot has a cut-off time for selection, beyond which the slot becomes unavailable. At cut-off time, all the orders to be delivered in the time slot are frozen. Every customer, based on her location, is assigned a hub from which her order would be shipped. So, at cut-off time, the operations controller (OC) at a hub knows how many orders need to be delivered in that upcoming slot. The OC then allocates these orders to a certain number of vans. Each van is allocated between 14–16 orders and follows a route. The route is created by the OC using the 'lat-long' data (short for latitude and longitude: the precise location co-ordinates of each customer). This is not as easy as it sounds because the OC does not know the size of each order and hence space required in the vans for the crates. So, some assumption has to be made about the volume an average order would occupy in the van.

Bigbasket had developed a process from day one for managing this using Google Maps and an interface where these details were available on a single screen. However, the quality of routing still depended on the OC and his knowledge of the area. We noticed some OCs did this very well compared to the others. And the same OC was not equally good on every day. Routing had to be completed within a tight time constraint. Only after the routing was completed could the orders be physically segregated into each van depending on what orders were in each route. As we started scaling and adding more hubs and cities, this manual routing clearly needed some automation.

Innovation in Routing

We could not find a single technology partner who could do both routing and tracking. We had to eventually pick two separate technology partners.

Immediately after the cut-off time, we would feed the routing vendor with both customer locations and the number of vans available at the hub along with the delivery slot timings. They would then take in all these data points and run their heavy algorithms and come up with routes.

On the tracking solution with Asset Trackr, we had to fit each delivery van with a physical device that could be monitored on its website. We started having frequent issues of device disconnection and damage. The device could only be repaired or refitted by an Asset Trackr engineer. That was turning out to be a challenge because their feet on the street were unable to keep pace with our rapid growth.

Single Routing and Tracking Solution

After having spent almost a year on this project, we decided to find an alternate solution. This time, we were clear that we wanted an integrated solution to both routing and tracking. We also wanted to partner with like-minded folks this time—a start-up that had a similar fire in the belly and wanted to grow along with us.

We zeroed in on a Bengaluru-based start-up called Locus. The solution they offered was good and we wanted to try it.

We did some trials and compared the routes that Locus generated with that of the previous technology partner. The routes that Locus generated were 20 per cent more optimal in terms of the distance the vans had to travel. This meant that the deliveries could be made more reliably within the time slot and also resulted in lower transportation costs. From a licensing costs perspective too, this solution was lighter on our wallet. We signed the deal with Locus.

Challenges on the Ground Were Plenty

We realised that each transshipment hub in our country was located at different distances from target customers, so we had to set a specific start time for the vans that varied by hub.

Next, the size of the vans varied significantly. We had Tata Aces, which could fit 75 crates and Maruti Ecos in Delhi that could carry only 35 crates.

We also realised that there was a service time which was not uniform across orders, as there were some orders with 1 crate or ₹200 ticket size and others with 10 crates with a ticket size of ₹5,000. So, we had to assign an appropriate time to each order size. We also realised orders with cash on delivery or any form of pay on delivery needed some additional time for service.

Indian cities are not all alike and neither are road conditions. In cities like Pune with a heavy military presence, there were road jammers on certain roads. In every city, there were one-way streets that were not updated on Google Maps. India was a nation under construction. There were hundreds of road diversions in every city. Google didn't seem to know about most of them. Locus tackled these by building a layer on top of their base solution and laying down restrictions on the map.

The number of orders that could be routed for a van also depended on the productivity of the CEE, which in turn depended on his tenure in the company. The churn of delivery personnel was high, and the pace at which we were growing ensured that at any point of time there would be anywhere between 20–40 per cent new employees. The newer ones had almost 30 per cent lower productivity than the more experienced ones. We addressed this by telling the Locus algorithm that certain vans would have lower productivity and hence a lesser number of orders had to be assigned to these routes.

Another requirement from hub staff was that some orders which were shifted from one slot to another after route generation had to be auto-adjusted into existing routes. This was also enabled by a button, which the OC would press, and these orders would be fed into nearby routes where van space and delivery time were available.

We even began creating routes based on the time of the day since traffic conditions vary. This fine-tuning resulted in a 2 per cent reduction in distance travelled. This was not a saving to be sniffed at given our scale of operations.

What started as a typical transportation algorithm now has features and configurations to represent the reality of cities, hubs and resource profiles. It has been a humongous task in getting the optimal solution and also getting our execution teams' approval. As one would expect, execution teams were not so enthusiastic in the initial phase since they did not see much benefit; on the other hand, they saw auto-routing as an unnecessary imposition—a classic case where a success of a strategic initiative needed lot of communication, trials and pilots, demonstrating quick wins, and, therefore, proof-points. Execution teams initially argued that manual routing is better since an experienced human who has a complete understanding of local conditions is doing this. They were sensing a loss of control in auto-routing. The Process team argued that manual execution is neither optimal nor scalable, and hence auto-routing is the way forward. We even had some regional business heads wanting to opt out of this, as the drivers refused to follow a given route. The transportation vendors' payout was now dependent on kilometres dictated by this software. But, there was light at the end of the tunnel. There was a lot of education and communication along with proof of the benefits. The whole system is now running like a well-oiled machine.

All's well that ends well, as they say. Locus gave us what we wanted. Routes within 20 minutes, creating shortest routes in the shortest time possible.

Auto-routing was a very long-drawn and interesting process initiative with lots of original thinking and development. There was a lot of drama at every step, but superior logic won at the end of the day. Even the most well-intentioned strategies can't guarantee execution success unless there is a clear buy-in from all stakeholders, with proper communication and robust programme management. And finally, all this was possible due to the analytics and AI-based learning that Locus brought to the table.

The Start of the Journey

Process excellence had a long history at Bigbasket, and laid a strong foundation in defining basic processes with emphasis on customer experience and gaining their trust. Towards the end of 2013, Bigbasket was looking at strengthening the delivery operations, especially in view of the expansion into new cities. At that time, Bigbasket had operations only in Bengaluru, Hyderabad and Mumbai.

Customer Experience Has Been the Central Pivot

When we say customer experience (CX) is at the centre of all processes at Bigbasket, it is not a cliché. All strategic and process decisions related to customer touch points, namely, web-app, physical product flow and delivery at the customer's home are contact centre technologies and are all always checked for their impact on CX. Even if a change could remotely affect CX, the change was not accepted. The commitment of the founders to CX has been covered in the chapter titled 'An Extra Pair of Shoes'.

CX is continually measured and feedback taken to find ways to improve and reduce friction at customer interface. Here is an example. Previously, the CEE's delivery app had a feature whereby a customer needed to key in a four-digit code to confirm delivery of an order. The CEE would hand over the delivery phone to the customer for her to key in this code that is known only to the customer. We realised that this was not always working. The customer who actually placed the order, who knew the code, may not be at home to receive the order when it was delivered. Also, some customers were not comfortable taking the phone from CEE for various reasons. In some rare cases, a few CEEs somehow got to know the code and tampered with the process. This feature, although well-intentioned, invariably created some friction. We removed this feature and instead found alternate ways of delivery confirmation.

In our customer support function, we don't have an Interactive Voice Response (IVR) like most companies. We wanted to give a quick human connect to customers who were trying to reach us. Our goal was to connect a customer to a human within 10 seconds 98 per cent of the time. We also took a decision to keep every customer support ticket open for 72 hours so that the agent had the context of any previous call or interaction in that time period. We also took the decision to provide an integrated view of all channels (calls, chats, emails and social media posts) in one interface for a customer support agent so that she could get a holistic picture.

Customer Support at Bigbasket Is Unique

Customer Support at Bigbasket is a key element of overall execution. If customers need to reach Bigbasket for any issue, be it a delivery delay, a quality issue noticed at the time of delivery or after delivery, they have multiple channels to reach us: call, email or chat. A few customers choose social media to report their issue and the relevant team spots and tracks these complaints to closure.

Bigbasket provides support for all interactions through any of these channels with a single system. We have chosen a cloud-based telephony solution for handling calls and a separate Customer Relationship Management (CRM) to look at the ticketing and customer interaction history. These two work seamlessly.

Customer Support grew from 30 members in early 2014 to over 1,200 now with four centres.

The story of how Bigbasket made the decision on the CRM solution makes for an interesting case study. When Bigbasket started, we were using a basic CRM with some customisations; it was called BPM 360 and it had limitations to customisation. And as we were scaling up, the complexities grew further, so much that BPM 360 could not meet our requirements anymore.

That is when we decided that it was time to change our CRM vendor, as all efforts to make this happen with the current vendor were in vain. After spending countless hours trying to work our way around the existing CRM solution, we were clear about what we needed from a new solution.

This was discussed internally and it was agreed that any new CRM vendor should be capable of handling most of the tasks with Application Programming Interface (API) linkages. The team also realised that it was a challenging task and it needed good programme management. A programme manager was appointed immediately for the CRM vendor selection, customisation effort and the subsequent integration with the rest of the Bigbasket systems.

Word spread in the market that Bigbasket was looking for a CRM vendor. The team started getting calls from vendors willing to demonstrate their products. There were a lot of young companies who were showcasing their products and the big boys of the industry also reached out to us.

We had learnt our lessons from our selection of the routing and tracking technology. It was important to find a technology partner who was customer-centric and had the same fire in the belly we had, and whose success would be tied to the implementation of their solution at Bigbasket.

We had set some eligibility criteria to the features and functionalities as a means of filtering vendors who were interested:

- Flexibility in customisation of the CRM as per our needs. This also involved the architectural change or change at the code level.
- It should be omni-channel.
- Easy to integrate with our existing applications such as cloud telephony and our back-end enterprise resource planning (ERP).

With the above parameters in mind, when we started evaluating the CRM vendors, we were able to filter a lot of them and were left with few vendors who had the potential to meet our requirements.

We then finally narrowed down to two CRM vendors:

- A large Chennai-based CRM vendor (CBV)
- Kapture

Learning from the Evaluation Process

This is neither about the large CBV nor about Kapture. This is about how we approached the whole evaluation process, what we looked for and finally how we made the decision.

CBV was one of the strongest players in this segment with a very good reputation in the market. On the other hand, Kapture was a young and dynamic company. Both had strong products.

Considering the product reputation of CBV, the team decided to evaluate it first. We met the CBV team at their office in Chennai. We were introduced to the Product team and told that they would also be joining the demo.

The demo started at 10 AM and in half an hour they ran the Bigbasket team through all the features and capabilities. The Bigbasket team then explained the workflows to the CBV team along with the underlying logic and how we wanted the customer interactions to be handled and stored. We always wanted all our customer interactions to be part of a single ticket (ticket is a unique folder where every interaction with a particular customer is stored). This helps the customer service representative to view the customer's past interaction-history at one glance.

The CBV team carefully listened to the requirements. After lunch, when the CBV team began explaining how our workflows would be handled by their system, it became evident that they were pushing Bigbasket to take their product as is. The CBV system did not have the ability to create the ticket upfront when a customer called or mailed us. They were requesting Bigbasket to modify our requirements, which included reassessing some of our fundamental process requests. They kept suggesting that we train our CS representatives to create tickets when needed. At this point, the Bigbasket team realised that this is a compromise that they couldn't afford to make. CBV were clearly not willing to customise the CRM to our needs.

Next week, we met the Kapture team. Those who had come for the demo included Sheshgiri, CEO of Kapture, and Vikas Garg, CTO, along with their Pre-sales team. The discussion was energising. Most of the time was spent in understanding our requirements through a consultative process of asking questions and probing deeper, with very little spent on selling their product. After understanding our requirements well, they assured us that all of it was doable.

Seeing our skepticism, Sheshgiri offered to build one workflow in their system and demo it to us.

When they presented the demo on 31 March 2016, the Bigbasket team was blown away. At the end of the presentation, they were convinced that this was the CRM they were looking for.

The final decision to go with Kapture was taken after a conference call where the team presented the relative merits of the two solutions to a larger group. For the first time at Bigbasket, a development of this nature was accomplished with minimal effort from the in-house Technology team.

Over the last three years, Kapture CRM lived up to its promise and scaled to meet our increasing load. Bigbasket has been able to add a number of features to improve customer experience. Kapture went on to support a number of new modules and features that allowed conducting and recording surveys, a knowledge management portal and a learning portal, among many others.

Customer Support at Bigbasket has a lot of other unique features. For example, if a customer has two more interactions on a complaint ticket and the issue still remains unresolved, the third interaction is handled by a senior customer support executive. We also call customers who have rated us low on an order delivery. Customer support function also supports marketing-related out-calling surveys.

One more important differentiator for Bigbasket's Customer Support function is that it also doubles up as an operations support centre. Whenever any CEE in the field faces an issue—inability to locate the address, customer unavailability, payment issues—he calls the Customer Support on a separate number and he is immediately connected to a separate set of agents trained in handling operations calls. This is done to ensure that customers are immediately taken into confidence on delivery issues and their concurrence taken just in case an order needs to be re-scheduled.

In Conclusion

Bigbasket's delivery operations and customer support are the two important legs of overall customer experience. We see this consistently in the Net Promoter Score (NPS) surveys, where the biggest driver is the quality of delivery experience.

A strong empathy for the customer and a belief in process has given muscle to these two legs of customer experience.

13
Order at the Edge of Chaos

Confidence comes from discipline and training.
—Robert Kiyosaki

Bigbasket had been meticulous in defining and developing processes around every aspect of customer delight. One example of such attention to the minutest detail was about how a CEE (more commonly referred to as a delivery person) had to open crates at a customer's home. Every order was packed in crates to prevent items getting messed up. You couldn't pack toilet cleaners with food items, for instance. So, each category of products was delivered in crates with different colours. And each crate was sealed with finely ribbed plastic cords similar to what some airlines use for sealing baggage. Before departing from the hub, to make deliveries, every CEE had to wrap a pouch around his waist. The pouch had a small cutter, among other things. The cutter had to be used to cut the plastic cords from the crates. After cutting the cords, they had to be put back into the crates and not discarded at the customer's premises. When Bigbasket began growing rapidly, we noticed that most delivery executives did not carry cutters. They opened the crates by just ripping open the crate covers. In the process, they ended up damaging the crates, dropping the plastic cords on the floor and creating a shoddy experience for customers.

Irrespective of what we did, we realised that we could not seem to assure adherence to this process, and many other similar processes, with a 'six sigma' kind of precision. The core value proposition was not impacted by not adhering to this process, but consistent adherence to the minutest process was what created customer delight and good word-of-mouth conversation.

After some discussion in the management council, we figured out that the process teams needed to be supported by a rigorous training framework and regime. So, we decided to hire a national training head who could help us drive this.

Hiring Our National Training Head

Our requirement was clear. Most folks in training operate at a stratospheric level doing exotic stuff like talent development and competency mapping. Dive a little deep and they would be clueless on what these terms really mean or how they could be seamlessly woven into solving real-world problems. We didn't want to hire someone who would come and tell us, 'I know how to conduct assessment centres, or I am a certified neuro linguistics trainer. I can do these for you.' Instead, we wanted someone who would come and ask us, 'Could you explain to me some of the business problems you have been facing? It would help me figure out the right training interventions.' We wanted someone who was hands-on and deeply understood the role training played in delivering consistent customer experience. We wanted someone who had a keen appreciation that scaling had an inherent tendency to wreck process adherence. On top of all this, we needed someone who could learn rapidly and take training to the next level as Bigbasket scaled. I (Hari) met at least 15 candidates before coming across the perfect person for this role. The person who demonstrated a strong belief that training needed to address real business problems was Neelam Ahluwalia.

It was November 2015 when we met Neelam at the Bigbasket office in Indiranagar. She came in for the meeting wearing a thick sweater. Winter hadn't even commenced in Bengaluru, and most people found even the peak winter weather there quite pleasant. We would later realise that anything below 25 degrees Celsius was cold for Neelam and below 23 degrees meant it was bone-chilling cold.

Neelam had done some good work at Flipkart and Narayana Hrudayalaya. She had a pattern of ending up in places where she had to set things up from scratch. She had grown up wanting to be a teacher, but her father had decided that she should be a chartered accountant. In between her articleship, she had got married. She soon had a dialogue with her husband, Rajesh, which she had found difficult with her rather tough dad. Rajesh convinced her dad that teaching and training was Neelam's calling and it didn't make sense for her to continue with her articleship.

Neelam has a no-nonsense demeanour, is extremely entrepreneurial, down-to-earth and strong on process measurement without an iota of fluff. She wanted to know what kind of a team she would inherit. I (Hari) told her we had small ragtag training outfits in the regions and had no corporate training function. One of her first jobs would be to create the right structure and build out these teams. She didn't seem to be deterred by this. On the contrary, she was excited. She was also impressed by the meetings she had with Balakumar, our operations head, and Hari Menon.

Neelam decided to come on board. That was the start of our journey in creating a strong and mature Training function.

First Things First

Within a week of joining Bigbasket, Neelam figured out that while processes had been meticulously defined, most of the training happened through a buddy mechanism where a senior CEE trained a new one. Process updates were not reliably disseminated, and basic soft skills like greeting a customer and dealing with women and senior citizens were imparted very inconsistently.

At the scale that Bigbasket had operated until then, this approach had worked reasonably well. But gradually, the cracks were beginning to show: customer complaints were on the rise, productivity was low and deliveries did not match invoices, among others.

And Bigbasket was growing rapidly. There were plans to hire another 4,000 associates in the next 12 months.

Along with the process heads and some members of the management council, Neelam worked out a strategy for addressing these gaps. She took two important decisions:

- Phase 1 of the training plan would focus on associates at the bottom of the pyramid. These were people who interacted directly with customers or performed activities that directly impacted customer experience. This was where there would be bang for the buck. Phase 2 would focus on strengthening the capability at the supervisory level. These were people who managed the associates; and finally, Phase 3 of the plan would address leadership development.
- Our approach to learning would be practical. Since 70 per cent of all real learning happened on the job, we would create these opportunities in a systematic way and equip managers with simple tools to do this every day.

Starting with Role-based Training

There was some content for associates, but it varied from region to region. There was no consistency, updates or revisions. Besides associates, for whom there was at least a semblance of content however motley or shabby, for the other role holders there was no structured content at all.

Towards the end of January 2016, all the trainers and training managers from the regions were called to the corporate office to fix some of these gaps.

Three teams were formed and each was given a set of roles for which they had to create structured training content. Once that was completed, input and final sign-off from the Process team were sought and finalised.

This was followed by setting up simulation labs in each region, with dummy machines, expired products, crates, etc., to give the trainees a look and feel of things on the floor.

There was the usual resistance to change. Operations felt that their current method of using senior role holders to train the new joiners worked well because there was no wastage of time in training. There was even more resistance when Neelam proposed certification of trainees before they were cleared for being put on the job. Between Neelam and Balakumar they were able to convince the regions that these changes were necessary as Bigbasket scaled. With this, role-based training was launched.

It had taken almost six months of persistence to have this implemented consistently across the regions.

Continuous Training Through Refreshers

After some debate in the leadership team, we took the call of soliciting feedback from customers on our CEEs through push notifications. Feedback was categorised under a few heads and there was space for some free text as well. With the help of our Analytics team, we looked through reams of free text to understand the overall customer sentiment and other behavioural issues with our CEEs. With timely feedback, some of the issues vanished overnight.

For non-customer facing employees like our warehouse staff, we measured efficiency and accuracy.

Based on these parameters for the warehousing staff, and customer feedback for the CEEs, we identified the bottom 30 per cent every month. These individuals, with special focus on the bottom 10 per cent, were put through intense refresher training. The top 10 per cent were invited to come to some of these refresher sessions and talk about what they did differently.

A simple Pareto showed that 10 per cent of the CEEs were contributing to 70 per cent of the problems. With this data, we targeted improvement programmes for these 10 per cent and this helped us optimise our training efforts.

Creativity in Content

Great content has always been central to training and the world was changing in the way it consumed content. The nature and quality of content could make or break any training intervention. So, we decided to hire someone who was good at content creation, had some experience in instructional design and had a good handle on the new ways in which the millennials consumed content.

That is how Anagha Karvir came on board. Besides being a creative designer, she is also a passionate Kathak dancer and plays the guitar. Since her joining, Anagha has helped create pulsating sound and light shows for the annual function.

Anagha's creativity complemented Neelam's process centricity. She led the charge on Phase 1 of the plan. Ineffective PowerPoint presentations were replaced by videos. She got the best training manager from the regions, Gangadhar, to supervise the shooting. Gangadhar himself starred in these videos. Right from converting the standard operating procedures (SOPs) to storyboards and then into lights and angles, Anagha managed it all. It was an arduous process. The videos were dubbed into several regional languages. She got the Process team to sign off, and the videos were ready to launch.

One evening on her way back home in a car pool with Deepti Sarma and Abhijeet Vulapu of the Technology team, Anagha got to know of a new tool that they were using for prototyping and testing user experience for iOS and Android apps. This tool, Canvas Flip, was available for free. Through Canvas Flip, different screens could be stitched together to create a simulation of real-life experience, which was awesome, and the navigation simple and intuitive. She spotted an opportunity here.

The very next day, Anagha called Amogha, an instructional designer in the Training team, and asked him to seriously evaluate transitioning the training content on the Bigbasket app from PowerPoint to Canvas Flip. Amogha is one of those rare gems who grew up in a small town without access to any privileged education, but made the best of what life had to offer. Today, thanks to him, Bigbasket trainees can walk into any classroom, scan the QR code for their respective role and log in to Canvas Flip to learn, without any assistance.

On to Supervisory and Leadership Training

By the end of July 2016, the content and execution of training for associates had firmly fallen in place. While the region Training teams ensured that the ball was not dropped on process training, Neelam turned her attention to developing an approach and content for the supervisors and managers. Anagha had done this at her last job and was eager to have a go at it.

We decided to build almost all the content in-house. The examples we used were all from the Bigbasket context that the participants could relate to. We branded this supervisory programme as L@BB (Leading at Bigbasket). To start with, it was a bouquet of five programmes, with two to three to be added every year. For us, L@BB had to solve real problems. It could not be a feel-good kind of a programme. Every module was carefully thought through and had to impart knowledge and skills that would make supervisors and first-line managers better at what they were expected to do every day. The modules were identified after discussing with several stakeholders on the ground. We decided on the following five programmes to start with:

- Roles of a manager
- Five habits of highly effective start-up employees
- Interviewing skills
- Managing conflict
- Managing a team

For the senior leadership team, we took a call to outsource all interventions. We looked around for some good partners who could help our leaders develop better self-awareness and become effective coaches. Today, a two-day leadership programme is a part of all quarterly business meets. Our leaders look forward to these programmes now. After self-awareness and coaching skills, they went through situational leadership, Myers–Briggs Type Indicator personality inventory, mindful leadership, execution focus and building high performance teams, among others.

In Conclusion

A lot of ground has been covered, but Neelam feels it is just the beginning.

It is normal human tendency to circumvent a difficult process when there are no consequences. Neelam put together a strong audit mechanism to ensure that what was prescribed in the manual was actually delivered on the ground. Every day with every batch of trainees.

The trainers themselves had to go through a process of periodic certification. Only if they cleared the certification process would they be eligible to do their job. Otherwise, they were pulled out for quick refreshers.

A wise person had once said, 'Sixty years ago I knew everything; now I know nothing; education is a progressive discovery of our own ignorance.' One could say the same thing about training as much as education. Any process is as good as the person behind it. And any person is as good as the training she has been through.

14
Love and Loyalty

We do not claim to be more unselfish, more generous or more philanthropic than other people. But we think we started on sound and straightforward business principles, considering the interests of the shareholders our own, and the health and welfare of the employees, the sure foundation of our prosperity.

—Jamsetji Tata

Santanu Paul, the founder of TalentSprint, and a keen commentator on technology and skills, was once telling me (Hari) that the good days of IT services may be soon coming to an end. This industry which had become an employment generation machine for the educated middle-class in the last three decades, was witnessing a slowdown. Several tasks that were performed manually were being automated. It is widely perceived that this industry may not see any net addition of jobs.

In contrast, there will be a growth in the number of jobs at the bottom and the top of the pyramid. Jobs in deep technology, AI, analytics and data sciences are opening up much faster than talent can be produced and trained to do these jobs. And in exactly the same fashion, the demand for jobs at the bottom of the pyramid has been outstripping supply. While the middle of the pyramid has been under the onslaught of automation, there has been a flood of jobs at the top and bottom of the pyramid.

The historic aspiration for education over skills in India has played out in interesting ways. It has helped India create middle- and high-end of the pyramid capabilities (space exploration, rocket science, information technology, etc.). The machinery and infrastructure needed at the lower end of the pyramid to lubricate the wheels of the economy have not received adequate attention and have grown creaky. The demand-supply dynamic is now rapidly revealing that most new jobs that will be created in the future need more of skills rather than rote education. Will this diminish the craze for a degree and rote education? Will this create a renewed impetus for skills? Our hypothesis is, 'Yes, it will.' Therefore, it is likely that the push for developing skills will be driven by the evolving nature of the job market rather than anything else.

E-commerce in India has contributed to a significant growth in jobs at the bottom of the pyramid. This has also given a big boost to skill development. Nothing is a better driver of skill development than demand driven by market forces.

TeamLease, one of India's large staffing companies, projects that the domestic e-commerce sector—among the fastest-growing globally—will employ 1 million delivery personnel by 2022, up from about 200,000 in 2017. Bigbasket itself has grown exponentially from employing 8,000 blue-collared workers in 2015 to 18,000 by the end of the financial year in 2019. While the absolute numbers are still miniscule in comparison to the number of young people entering employable age each year in India, it is true that e-commerce will be one of the big engines of employment generation in the years to come.

Baluben Parmar and Shamsher Alam

Baluben Parmar had an unhappy childhood and a difficult life as an adult. In typical lower middle-class Indian tradition, her parents had her married at a young age. Her husband passed away less than 10 years after marriage leaving her with three young children to look after. She worked as a domestic help and barely earned enough to make ends meet.

Bigbasket had begun operations in Ahmedabad and was looking for people in various functions. Someone she knew worked at Bigbasket and asked her to apply for an opening. She applied and got a job in the housekeeping section. She tells anyone who would care to listen that Bigbasket had given her a new lease of life. She is respected and cared for. She also earns enough to educate her children and save for their future.

Shamsher Alam was one of the many unemployed young men living in Kolkata. He was a school dropout with no employable skills. He spent his days doing petty jobs and hanging around with the other unemployed youth in the neighbourhood. Lack of a steady income continues to haunt a majority of the employable youth in India. Out of the total workforce of 520 million people, only 85 million—or one in six—are regular salaried employees. And, out of this, only 12 million are estimated to be regular salaried employees where labour laws are strictly enforced.

One day, Shamsher got to know from a friend that Bigbasket was hiring delivery boys. When he got to know the salary offered, and an opportunity for permanent employment, he was excited enough to give it a shot. The salary on offer was modest, but was a lot for someone who did part-time jobs and went in and out of employment as a way of life.

Shamsher turned up for the interview wearing clothes borrowed from his friend since he didn't have a presentable attire. His honest answers and his attitude impressed Swarnarekha Roy. Swarnarekha was the training manager at Kolkata and was one of those individuals who had grown up having a soft corner for the underdog. Shamsher has now completed three years at Bigbasket and thinks of the company as his second family. He always goes beyond his call of duty and is ready to lend a helping hand wherever it is needed.

However, the bitter truth is that a majority of the blue-collar workforce is not as happy and fulfilled as Baluben Parmar or Shamsher Alam.

With their upbringing steeped in financial and personal problems, most of them have had hard lives. The income from their jobs is not sufficiently attractive to hold them for long in an urban setting where the cost of living is high. Limited career growth opportunities only add to the tenuousness of their relationship with the company they work for. Therefore, a slight pull or a nudge is enough to make them abscond or quit. The nudge can be a rude remark from their supervisor or excess workload during a peak day.

We have realised that basic respect for human dignity, which we all take for granted, is what they crave the most. And when they don't get it, some of them could turn rude. For every instance of rude behaviour, we have also found some extraordinary display of human values. Shrikant Vasant Supugade was delivering a customer order in Borivali, Mumbai, when the customer's aged mother-in-law suffered a paralytic attack. The customer panicked. Shrikant kept his cool and immediately called up an ambulance. He waited until the ambulance arrived and carried the patient to the vehicle and accompanied her to the hospital. His timely action saved the patient from certain death.

The increasing competition in e-commerce and food-tech for such talent has resulted in high attrition rates across industry. But frankly, we believe that the increasing demand for this category of workforce is a good thing. So far, only talent in the technology sector could call the shots, but it is good to see how a free market can offer this privilege to those at the bottom of the pyramid as well, and in the process, uplift their living standards.

Our attempts to curb attrition, and earn their loyalty, did not just stem from the impact attrition in this category of workforce has on our operations. It was a deeper belief that it is important to do the right thing from a human perspective. In all likelihood, it would help stabilise our operations, but even if it did not, it would not detract us from doing the right thing.

Reinventing the wheel may be a waste of time, but sometimes going through the whole process and experiencing the reality keeps you grounded and gives you confidence. We re-discovered that four things are truly important in earning the love and loyalty of this category of workforce, namely, hiring correctly, training them and supporting them in the early phase, treating them with respect and rewarding them for good work, and paying them a fair wage.

Hiring Right

We look for four things in a candidate. Does the individual demonstrate good attitude and is he/she trainable? Does this individual demonstrate respect for women and senior citizens? Does this person have a tendency to be uncivil or rude? Does the individual have elementary personal hygiene and grooming standards?

Even the best processes tend to break down at scale. The selection process and the way the filters operated would also break down from time to time and had to be reinforced by a stringent audit process.

Hiring correct was half the problem solved.

Hiring has been a constant challenge in the cities. Therefore, we are tying up with local governments and panchayats to reach out to the rural population. Using the 'gig economy' to our advantage, we now also work with freelance bikers who deliver orders for us and get paid per order, aside from permanent and contract employees.

Training and Support

Process training is the Holy Grail of Bigbasket. The Training team along with Operations has painstakingly put together a comprehensive set of modules, which covers each step of the value chain, no matter how small or seemingly uncomplicated it may appear. The training process is strictly followed right from induction of new joiners. All associates who join Bigbasket must go through a mandatory New Hire Training (NHT), after which they are certified, and only then allowed to start work in the live environment. However, it doesn't stop there. As mentioned before, the bottom 10 per cent of performers are taken through refresher training and their performance is strictly monitored till they reach acceptable standards.

We have increasingly observed that nearly 70 per cent of attrition among the associates is attributable to new joiners leaving us within the first 60 days. This became a major problem for our current and future growth plans and led to a companywide assessment through engagement surveys and focused group discussions to get to the root cause. We found out that a large chunk of our new joiners who come from rural India are so overwhelmed by new processes, workload and the work environment that they can't cope up and leave.

A programme was designed to handhold the new joiners by assigning a group of them to a mentor of sorts—Team Lead (TL). TLs would be a cross between a senior colleague and an on-the-job trainer. They would be responsible for complete handholding of the new associates for the first 60 days, and gradually get them up to speed. An incentive plan for the TLs was also put in place to create the right motivation. Only the top performing associates were chosen as TLs after they cleared screening rounds that assessed them for helpfulness, likeability and honesty. This initiative was aptly named Neev, the Sanskrit word for foundation. Neev has been received well by the new joiners. Early indications are that it is having a positive outcome.

Rewarding Good Work

We have always believed in rewarding good work. The top 30 per cent of associates in each region are recognised every month and rewarded for their performance. However, this became routine after a while and lacked the 'oomph'. It did not generate excitement and a healthy competition amongst the employees.

Bigbasket celebrates its Annual Day, 'Breaking Barriers', with great pomp and show. Every year the organising committee, headed by Balakumar, tries to make this event as engaging as possible. Amidst preparations for the festivities for 2018, Balakumar and Tanuja were brainstorming on a Recognition programme for our associates that would really show the awardees the appreciation Bigbasket had for their hard work and also serve as an experience that other associates could aspire for. Thus, the initiative 'BB Rockstar' was conceived.

The selection process was designed to assess the associates on their alignment to our values and culture along with productivity. Top 30 associates from across the country were flown to the corporate office of Bigbasket in Bengaluru to attend the Annual Day, where they were all called upon stage amidst thunderous applause. They were also provided a platform to interact with the senior leadership team and were encouraged to be openly expressive of things that were going well and areas that needed improvement.

The BB Rockstar concept was a huge hit and the leadership decided to institutionalise it by making it a biannual event. One would be held in Bengaluru at Breaking Barriers in April and the other to be held locally in October. The regional business heads took it upon themselves to rival the corporate office in making it a grand show. They even invited the families of the Rockstars and made it a day for them to remember. Members from the senior leadership team visited all locations to commend the winners.

After this initiative, the Rockstars have become celebrities in their regions with some special privileges like opportunities to mentor new joiners and faster career progression. We wanted the other associates to look up to the Rockstars.

Treating Employees with Respect

Sometime in 2015, Bigbasket set up a Trust for the blue-collar workforce. Benefits under this Trust included enhancing education and skill levels of the associates and helping them in their quest for upward social mobility. Any associate who had spent more than 12 months at Bigbasket was eligible for educational assistance (reimbursement for school and college fees, text books, etc.) for themselves and their families. The benefits also included liberal insurance cover. The benefits were available to associates who worked at Bigbasket irrespective of whether they were on our own rolls or that of a third party. This initiative won us the TRRAIN (Trust for Retailers & Retail Associates of India) HR Initiative of the Year award in 2018. Awards do not mean much, but sometimes you feel the pride in your heart when an award recognises you for something you've given your heart and soul to.

Through the Trust, we have also tied up with expert organisations like LabourNet, which help our associates identify right vocational courses that could enhance their employability and create jobs for their dependents.

Treating everyone with respect is easier said than done. Respect often breaks down under stress. On peak days when order flow is high, there is some stress at all levels. The stress gets passed down and is manifested in rude behaviour and foul language. We have conducted training for all our supervisors who interact with associates on what is unacceptable behaviour. We had noticed that supervisors routinely turned down legitimate requests for leave by citing work pressure as one of the reasons. This encouraged associates to abscond without information. We took away this discretion by automating this whole process where a denial of a legitimate leave request would now have to be signed off by the function head.

We conducted the first Employee Satisfaction Survey for our blue-collared workforce this year. The questions were tailor-designed to get a feel of the pulse on the ground. The questionnaire was translated into regional languages and circulated amongst the employees. We were expecting to do okay, as we had always designed HR policies, processes and benefits keeping in mind simplicity, transparency and relevance.

But, we also knew that framing policies from the ivory tower of the corporate office is easy. The execution on the ground, day after day, was what really mattered. So, we waited for the results with bated breath.

We were pleasantly surprised and relieved with the outcome. The average score of 4.12 on a 5-point scale validated what we believed. Further, the NPS equivalent question (I will recommend Bigbasket as a great place to work) got an average score of 4.4 from a maximum of 5 points, which blew us away. It was clear that the actions that we had taken towards employee welfare were working and we were on the right track.

The Employee Satisfaction Survey had highlighted infrastructure and amenities as an area of improvement. We did not waste any time and immediately chalked out a standard checklist for all locations and implemented it within a month.

Diversity and Inclusion at This Level

Environments that promote diversity and inclusion have historically been more effective at promoting innovation and excellence than those that don't. Bollywood, Bengaluru, the US and Hollywood are outstanding examples at a macro level.

With the goal of enhancing diversity, increasing productivity and reducing attrition, we piloted the first batch of women pickers at our warehouse in Pune. Picking was a predominantly male bastion. Therefore, before the first batch of women pickers joined us, we had enrolled the entire male workforce to a gender sensitivity course. They were taught the basic dos and don'ts. Separate sessions were also taken on the Bigbasket policy of Prevention of Sexual Harassment @ Workplace to strictly reinforce our zero tolerance stand.

The women pickers have now rapidly caught up with their male counterparts. Currently, productivity is high and attrition is low for the women pickers. Maya Patil, a woman picker in Pune, loves coming to work even though she has a long commute. She says that working for Bigbasket has been a great experience and even though women like her are in the minority at the warehouse, she has always felt safe and respected. This has helped her give her best to her work. Following the success of this initiative, other regions have also started recruiting women pickers.

In Conclusion

Have we earned the love and loyalty of our associates? Have we cracked the attrition problem? We are not sure. If we go by the employee satisfaction results, maybe we have come some distance in this quest. Our goal is not to reduce attrition but to be the 'Employer of Choice' for our associates. On this journey, we have taken incremental steps to ensure that the associates are engaged by putting all hygiene factors in place, like on time and accurate salary disbursement, timely enrolment in Employee State Insurance plans, helping them and their families with the Trust, creating a safe workplace for women, creating a strong culture of service orientation and, above all, constant communication. Reduction in attrition is only a welcome by-product in the journey towards achieving this goal.

15
In Closing

The Universe is made of stories, not of atoms.

—Muriel Rukeyser

There is something very compelling about a story. It can romanticise the mundane and humdrum. A story also has the amazing capacity to leave you admiring and envying characters who, if you had actually met in real life, may have seemed ordinary and unworthy of desire. The flip side of this is that everything that seems mundane can actually be romantic and spectacular if you choose to look at it that way, and if you create and seed the right stories in your mind.

Life would be delightful and breathtaking, story-like, if you are happy with who you are; if you don't desperately seek endorsement or try to always fit in; if you don't worry a lot about being judged, and at the same time let others just be, without judging them. This holds true irrespective of whether you are an individual or a company.

In many ways this is the sum and substance of Bigbasket.

We thought it may help to summarise and highlight a few key takeaways. And these are not just coming from what we did well, but also from where we goofed up.

Stay grounded: All of us learn lessons in life and we should value them. While we need to be flexible, we should remain grounded and not be carried away by what's in vogue. This is one of the true tests of character. When the fad blows away, you will feel good about yourself and the fact that you didn't sway too much.

Don't lose the ability to be hands-on: The big picture is important but don't lose touch of the ground reality. It is common to see even the most accomplished professors teaching a basic course to the first year students at a university. This helps them stay grounded and in touch with fundamentals. This applies as much to leaders in companies as much to professors in universities.

Culture is important: People evaluate the culture of a place by seeing how leaders behave. A hundred CEO speeches on culture are not as good as demonstrated behaviour. So, ensure that you use all opportunities to showcase the culture you wish to create. Ensure that 10 of your colleagues do the same. There will be moments when you would want to take shortcuts. While shortcuts may be inevitable once in a while, be very careful about taking those that undermine the culture.

Always start with the 'why': It helps you define the problem better and will be your north star when you lose direction. And you are bound to lose direction periodically.

Delegate but keep track of the most important things: Pay personal attention to these. Most of the people who claim they don't have the time are often lost in the weeds. They are busy with things that someone in their team should be doing. They have not cared to build a team or coach their team members or empower them. As a result, the important things are neglected. Or they delegate so much that there is very little difference from abdication.

Define your talent strategy thoughtfully: Google might have benefited immensely by hiring hundreds of folks from top-notch universities at top salaries, but that may not be the best strategy for you. Here again, no strategy is right or wrong. Your business context and your personal beliefs are important.

Cut the crap and jargon: Technology and analytics are important but they are often overplayed. Don't ever stop asking basic questions; don't ever lose sight of first-principles thinking. Don't get carried away by jargon and geek-speak. Get the experts to speak a language that anyone with some clear thinking can understand. Be optimistic but have a healthy skepticism of hype. Ask a lot of questions. Question the status-quo. Ask, 'So what?' And ask what would happen if we remove some of our self-imposed constraints.

Some things are just good to do: As far as possible, define the outcomes you expect and evaluate whether your initiatives are delivering the outcomes you expected. But don't hesitate doing some fundamentally sound things even if outcomes cannot easily be measured in the short term. Treating people well, taking care of their welfare and security, creating safe work spaces and helping them do their jobs better will all qualify as fundamentally right things to do.

Differentiate good costs from bad costs: Be extremely frugal before the product-market fit has been established. Hire people who can multitask. Have people do overlapping roles if needed. Do not splurge on anything. Do not hire heavyweights unless absolutely necessary. Hire people who can punch above their weight class and those with a fire in the belly. Operate out of simple and functional facilities. However, after the product-market fit is established and you are in a growth mode, make the right investments in people and other resources. Get tools that enhance productivity. Operate out of facilities that can get teams face time. Lease or build facilities ahead of the curve so that teams do not get randomly dispersed across multiple and sub-optimal facilities. The intangible cost of this is just unbelievable. The cost of lost business can far exceed the cost of sub-optimal capacity utilisation. The intangible costs of having functions led by undersized leaders at this stage of growth can be high. This may not be very evident.

Process is important: If executed diligently even ordinary people can deliver extraordinary customer experience. It is human tendency, especially in an Indian context, to deviate from process the moment you take your eyes off. So, it is very important to ensure process adherence with a tight audit process and where there are consequences for process deviation.

Internal customer centricity: Internal customers are as important as external, paying customers. Some of your employees serve paying customers. The rest of them must serve these employees.

Avoid activity traps: Don't sponsor events because it is a good thing to do. Don't nominate people for expensive training programmes because it is considered the right thing to do. Don't do anything because it is considered good. These things act as conversation starters or talking points in social contexts, but may not yield bang for the buck. Activity traps can sap energy and focus. So, avoid activities that show you are doing something even if not doing anything may be the best thing.

We hope you enjoyed reading the book as much as we enjoyed writing it.

About the Authors

T.N. Hari is an advisor and sounding board to numerous young entrepreneurs and start-ups. He is also a strategic advisor at the Fundamentum Partnership and heads human resources at Bigbasket.

A graduate of IIT and IIM, Hari has worked at an executive level with multiple start-ups/scale-ups. He has been through four successful exits in different industries (Daksh, Virtusa, Amba Research and TaxiForSure).

His passion lies in scaling organisations through clear thinking and relentless execution. The co-author of three books (his last two published titles are *Cut the Crap and Jargon—Lessons from the Start-up Trenches* and *Cutting the Gordian Knot—India's Quest for Prosperity)*, Hari is also a prolific writer with a huge following. LinkedIn identified him as one of the Top Voices in India for three successive years (2016, 2017 and 2018).

M.S. Subramanian currently heads the analytics function at Bigbasket, with a focus on delivering definitive actionable insights that help enhance customer experience. With over 20 years of experience in analytics leadership, Mani has worked with companies such as Dell, McKinsey, Infosys, Ernst & Young and PwC.

An undergraduate engineering degree in computer science from the University of Madras, an MBA from IIM, Ahmedabad, and a graduate engineering degree in supply chain management from Massachusetts Institute of Technology (MIT), Mani is a frequent speaker in industry and academic forums as an analytics expert. Some of his recent events include speaker at AIMinds—the hub for AI Intellectuals, IIM Bangalore's Retail Master Class, panel moderator/member in industry forums (Cypher, SCPC), hands-on workshop in analytics at UpGrad and other forums. He has also been a part-time faculty member, delivering graduate-level analytics courses at Symbiosis Institute of Business Management (SIBM) and Narsee Monjee Institute of Management Studies (NMIMS) in Bengaluru.